Julian Baggini is the editor and co-founder of *The Philosophers' Magazine*. His books include *Do They Think You're Stupid?: 100 Ways of Spotting Spin & Nonsense from the Media, Pundits & Politicians*, *Welcome to Everytown: A Journey into the English Mind*, *What's It All About? – Philosophy and the Meaning of Life* and the bestselling *The Pig That Wants to be Eaten*, which has been translated into eighteen languages.

www.julianbaggini.com
www.microphilosophy.net

Also by Julian Baggini

*Do They Think You're Stupid?: 100 Ways of Spotting Spin &
Nonsense from the Media, Pundits & Politicians*

Welcome to Everytown: A Journey into the English Mind

The Pig That Wants to be Eaten

What's It All About? – Philosophy and the Meaning of Life

By Julian Baggini and Jeremy Stangroom

Do You Think What You Think You Think?

SHOULD YOU JUDGE THIS BOOK BY ITS COVER?

100 Fresh Takes on Familiar
Sayings and Quotations

JULIAN BAGGINI

GRANTA

Granta Publications, 12 Addison Avenue, London W11 4QR

First published in Great Britain by Granta Books, 2009
This paperback edition published by Granta Books, 2010

Copyright © Julian Baggini, 2009

A CIP catalogue record for this book
is available from the British Library.

1 3 5 7 9 10 8 6 4 2

ISBN 978 1 84708 155 1

Printed and bound in Great Britain by
CPI Bookmarque, Croydon

Contents

Contents

Contents

Contents

Preface

Asked what I thought about aphorisms, I once replied with one of my own: A person who has an aphorism for everything gives thought to nothing.

The best aphorisms, proverbs and sayings manage to encapsulate important ideas in few words. But they can be too beguiling. They trick us into thinking we've grasped a deep thought by their wit and brevity. Poke them, however, and you find they ride roughshod over all sorts of complexities and subtleties.

For example, an almost universal law of folk wisdom is that every proverb has an equal and opposite proverb. So, you can't teach an old dog new tricks, but then again, it's never too late. Great minds think alike, but one man's meat is another man's poison. Two heads are better than one, but too many cooks spoil the broth.

It is not that such oppositions cancel each other out, leaving us with nothing. It is rather that each saying captures only part of the truth. They lead us astray only when the realization that there is *something* in it slides into an assumption that there's *nothing not* in it.

My own aphorism was meant to both explain and exemplify the virtues and vices of well-worn proverbs, sayings and quotations. On the one hand, it is not literally true that a person who has an aphorism for everything gives thought to nothing. Nevertheless, I think it does neatly capture the danger of confusing having access to a store of wisdom and actually being wise yourself. A parrot which says nothing but the words of great minds does not itself possess one.

That is why I wanted to return to many of the wise words we ourselves parrot but without necessarily really thinking about them. Wisdom can mutate into folly when it is repeated without thought or reflection.

The French have a saying, *Proverbe ne peut mentir*: a proverb cannot lie. That's as maybe, but it can be misunderstood or abused so that it ceases to speak the truth. The aim of this book is to make proverbs and other familiar sayings speak their wisdom afresh, and to clear away some of the mistaken ideas they can give rise to.

In order to achieve this goal, it is important that I do not try to replace one set of pat interpretations with another. Rather, I want to stimulate the reader to think for herself about the ideas within, as if for the first time. That is why I do not attempt to make my discussions exhaustive. Nor do I spell everything out: the point is to make the reader check her own spelling.

The selection of phrases and quotations to compare and contrast should be read in this spirit. Sometimes their connection with the main discussion is obvious, on other occasions less so. Sometimes they hit the nail on the head, sometimes the hammer lands hard on the author's thumb. Likewise, there are overlaps and connections between many of the one hundred sayings which provide the focus for the book, and I trust the reader's capacity to notice and explore them herself.

This is a book to argue and converse with. It is not a reference book, manual or self-help guide. It exists simply to fuel the thinking of those who think for themselves.

1. A bird in the hand is worth two in the bush

Mid 15th century

Experiments show that a bird in the hand is actually perceived to be worth 2.48 in the bush. To be precise, the 'birds' were in fact coffee cups, but since the animals are merely proverbial, the general point still holds.

Experimenters divided a group randomly and gave half of them a coffee mug each. These were deemed 'sellers' while the others were cast in the role of buyers. Sellers were then asked how much they would be willing to part with the mug for, while buyers were asked how much they would pay for one. On average, buyers valued the mugs at no more than $2.87, while sellers valued them at $7.12. The mere fact that the sellers already had the mugs led them to perceive them as being much more valuable than they otherwise would.

This phenomenon, called loss-aversion, has been observed in countless other situations. However, it is completely irrational. This is made even clearer by another experiment which demonstrated the 'endowment effect'. This time, half a group received one item and half a group received a different one. Because the goods were distributed randomly, you would expect half the group to have received the item which was of less value to them personally. But when asked if they would be willing to trade, only between

10 and 30 per cent said they would do so. Again, ownership led people to over-value.

Of course, it is often better to keep what you have than risk it all for more, which is the proper moral of the proverb. But when there is no risk involved, we still tend to stick with what we have, even if it is in our interests to give it up. Two birds in a bush which are hard to catch may not be worth hunting if you already have one. But when they're just sitting there waiting to be picked up, it would be foolish to prefer the beast you already have. Yet experiments show such foolishness is a natural inclination we have to struggle to avoid.[1]

Compare and contrast

An egg today is better than a chicken tomorrow. *Italian proverb*

Better a sparrow in hand than a crane in flight. *French proverb*

A sparrow in the hand is better than a pigeon on the roof. *German proverb*

2

2. Manners maketh man

Bishop William Wykeham of Winchester
(1324–1404)

'Manners maketh man' was the personal motto of Bishop Wykeham, the founder of Winchester College, one of England's oldest public schools. The idea of a church leader placing such high importance on so trivial a notion as manners can strike us today as absurd. Manners are not morals, and even a little distance in time or space can show them to be arbitrary and petty.

Take, for instance, some of the advice in G. R. M. Devereaux's *Etiquette for Men: A Book of Modern Manners and Customs*, published in 1929. 'It is not necessary for you to raise your hat if you see a lady of your acquaintance in a public vehicle in which you are also a passenger,' he writes. 'Otherwise, you should always raise your hat when meeting a lady you know,' although 'you should avoid offering a lady your gloved hand'. He also describes a strict formula for who should be introduced to whom in social gatherings: gentlemen to men, single girls to married women, and young to older men. The most dated advice of all is, 'After a stay at a friend's house you should tip the servants.' Or perhaps I just have the wrong friends.

The idea that following customs such as these is the making of a man, or woman, seems quite preposterous.

However, one should not confuse changing customs with the enduring principles which underpin them. As Devereaux put it, 'Consideration for others at all times is the keynote of etiquette.'

Manners are indeed trivial if they are identified solely with local and changing practices. But if they are thought of in a broader sense, as a concern to treat others well, then they evidently are central to the ethics of everyday life.

If you think manners are of no interest to someone wishing to be a better person, consider the final sentence of Devereaux's etiquette guide: 'The finest way in which children can be trained to grow up into thoughtful, courteous and considerate men and women is by surrounding them with those qualities throughout their younger days.' A concern with manners can lead you to much more important matters than how to hold your fork.

Compare and contrast

Civility costs nothing. *Early 18th century*

He was born without pants and is ashamed to be dressed. *Greek proverb*

Good breeding consists in concealing how much we think of ourselves and how little we think of the other person. *Mark Twain (1835–1910)*

3. 'Tis better to have loved and lost / Than never to have loved at all

Alfred, Lord Tennyson (1809–92)

In a spin-off book to the comedy TV series *Not The Nine O'clock News*, Tennyson's sage words are rendered anew as 'It's better to have loved and lost than it is to spend your whole life wanking.'

The deliberate variation, apart from being very funny, transforms the original in two ways common misunderstanding can. First, of course, is the equation of love and sex. To have loved and lost is not the same as to have shagged and lost, though that too may be better than never to have shagged at all.

Second, and more significantly, it has the effect of transforming a consolation into an exhortation. Whether we remain life-long singletons or have even brief sexual relationships with others is something that we can, to a certain degree, control. If we think that even bad sex is preferable to masturbatory solitude, that can provide the spur to seek out some of the numerous others who feel the same way and would gladly take our companionship.

But although a sexual liaison can be a mutually convenient deal between consenting adults, love cannot be so easily arranged. We cannot just choose to fall in love. Believing it is better to have loved and lost does not make us any more likely to find love. Rather, the best time to hear such words is when love has gone, to help us come to terms with our loss.

There is, nevertheless, one sense in which heeding Tennyson's line from 'In Memoriam A. H. H.' can help prepare us for love, should it call. The message is not that any relationship is better than none at all. If we want to keep ourselves open to the possibility of a love worth losing, we need to retain at least a spark of romanticism. To truly believe we can love and lose requires belief that we can truly love.

Compare and contrast

Opportunity never knocks twice at any man's door. *Mid 16th century*

The world belongs to the bold. *Spanish proverb*

Not having shot is always to have missed. *Dutch proverb*

4. No smoke without fire

Late Middle Ages

Although people still frequently say that there is no smoke without fire, few believe this in their hearts to be a general truth. We know, for example, that much of the smoke that chokes the pages of the tabloid papers and celebrity gossip magazines comes from fires that burn only in the bellies of ambitious journalists. When someone says sincerely that there is no smoke without fire, it is usually because they are already convinced of the presence of flames, not because they really believe the refrain lends support to their suspicions.

Nevertheless, in a way, this tired old saying is cannier than at first may appear. It is, of course, patently false if we take it to mean that there is some truth in every rumour or scandal. But if we take its imagery a little more literally, another possibility suggests itself. You can indeed always infer the presence of fire from the appearance of smoke; what you may not know is the kind of fire it is, or whether it is already dying out.

So it is with gossip. It never emerges from a vacuum. If what started people's ears burning wasn't an accident or a natural spark, we know someone must have been making mischief with matches. The question is, who and why?

Take any story of celebrity rivalry. How much of the smoke this generates is the result of their actual disagreements and how much is being generated by genuine rivals and allies with vested interests in exaggerating the rift? No smoke without fire, to be sure. But where are the real fires blazing and who is fanning the flames?

We should not lazily assume that the connection between hearsay and truth is a straightforward one of cause and effect. Reading the smoke signals accurately requires us to look more closely at where they are really coming from. Look carefully and you might just find fires in unexpected places.

Compare and contrast

Throw dirt enough, and some will stick. *Mid 17th century*

Where wood is being chopped, shavings fly. *Polish proverb*

If the wind comes from an empty cave, it's not without a reason. *Chinese proverb*

5. Nothing in excess

Inscription on the Temple of Apollo at Delphi, 6th century BCE

An adviser can always be right yet not much use. For example, I am no agony uncle, yet I can offer guidance that I guarantee to be sound: when shopping, never buy anything that is too expensive. In love, do not marry the wrong person. And war is such a terrible thing that you must never, ever wage one unless not doing so is even worse.

The problem is that all these counsels are mere tautologies: they are true by definition. It takes no more than a basic grasp of the English language to realize that the wrong person, a war that is not right or a product that is 'too expensive' are all to be avoided. What we need to know is what makes someone an unsuitable spouse, a purchase too expensive or a war unjust.

The seven wise men who are supposed to have come up with the two wise words inscribed at Delphi, *Μηδεν Αγαν*, come close to being just as vacuous. For the injunction not to do anything to excess is also a tautology: an excess just is too much, and so by definition is already wrong. People who praise excess are really criticizing conventional ideas about what too much is. The difficulty lies in knowing how much is too much, not that too much is bad.

What is an excessive amount of alcohol, for example? For

a teetotaller it is one sip. For a driver, it is not much more than a glass. For a student in search of oblivion, excess is reached only when the alcohol in the bloodstream rises to toxic concentrations.

The Delphic command is not entirely empty, it's just rather modest in what it tells us. It merely offers a reminder that there is an appropriate level or quantity for everything and that we should be on our guards never to overstep the mark. Worthy advice, for sure. Whether it merits immortalization in sacred stone is another matter.

Compare and contrast

The last drop makes the cup run over. *Mid 7th century*

Enough is as good as a feast. *Late 14th century*

Coriander is good, but not too much. *Spanish proverb*

6. Jack of all trades and master of none

Early 17th century

Isaiah Berlin popularized a quotation attributed to the Ancient Greek poet Archilochus: 'The fox knows many things, but the hedgehog knows one big thing.' To ask which is better, the hedgehog or the fox, is to miss the point. Both beasts have their strengths and weaknesses.

Proverbial Jack is the fox felled by his lack of depth. But arguably, a bigger problem today is an infestation of sickly hedgehogs, all masters of one. Academic specialization, for example, has gone so far that two colleagues who are supposed to be experts in the same subject can have almost no knowledge in common. This matters because creativity about ideas requires making connections, and if you work only in one small area, you'll miss them.

Over-specialization can also be a problem at work. People on production lines doing just one job become bored and demoralized. Companies which make or do just one thing are vulnerable to collapses in markets or the arrival of vigorous competition.

At the same time, being a happy fox has never been easier. Technology means we can all be photographers, film makers and music makers now, without having to spend years mastering the tools of the trade.

If in some respects we are not enough like Jack, and in others quite right to be, is there any truth left in the saying at all? There is, and it's found in the word 'master'. To really excel at something, you need focus and dedication. More people can be decent photographers in a world of digital SLRs, but to be an excellent one, you still have to work at it. So the real question we should ask ourselves is, do we want to try to be masters of one thing (and perhaps fail) or would we prefer to be merely competent in many? All that Jack shows us is that this is indeed a choice. How we choose is an open question, but unless you're a Leonardo, choose you must.

Compare and contrast

Variety is the spice of life. *Late 18th century*

Perfection is the child of time. *Joseph Hall (1574–1656)*

The intellect of man is forced to choose / Perfection of the life, or of the work. *W. B. Yeats (1865–1939)*

7. No man is an island, entire of itself

John Donne (1572–1631)

One of the most profound jokes ever made is in *Monty Python's Life of Brian*, when the eponymous non-Messiah tells a crowd of worshippers 'You're all individuals.'

'Yes! We're all individuals!' they reply as one, apart from a man called Dennis who pipes up, 'I'm not.'

The joke captures the contradictions and paradoxes that emerge when we think about the nature of human individuality. At different times, we are drawn to different conclusions about how discrete we really are. Sometimes, it seems obvious that we are all of us interconnected and interdependent, and that 'no man is an island'. Yet at others, we would nod along with Marlow's line in Conrad's *Heart of Darkness*, agreeing that 'We live, as we dream alone.' So what are we really – fundamentally at one with others, or cut off from them?

Donne seemed to take his interconnectedness theory very seriously indeed. 'Any man's death diminishes me,' he wrote, 'because I am involved in mankind.' This seems to flatly contradict Marlow, but it also seems to be a romantic exaggeration. People are dying every second, often horribly, yet at such moments others are laughing, often at frivolous things. If the deaths of others always diminish us, it is to a degree we cannot even notice.

Take both claims less literally, however, and you can see how each captures a different facet of the human experience. We live life from the inside out, and no one, no matter how intimately we know them, can ever really get inside with us. In that sense, we are indeed alone. But very few can live entirely cut off from all others. Trapped though we are in our own selves, we often look outwards, and open up windows to each other so that we can share our experiences as much as is possible.

There is no contradiction here, merely a tension. We are social, public animals with individual, private subjectivities. We may not be islands, but there are still some boundaries between self and other which cannot be crossed.

Compare and contrast

He travels fastest who travels alone. *Late 19th century*

Better be alone than in bad company. *French proverb*

He who eats alone dies alone. *Italian proverb*

8. Forget and forgive

William Shakespeare (1564–1616)

Although forgiveness has been advocated as a virtue for most of human history, its coupling with forgetting is a much more recent development. In the Victorian era, former Prime Minister Arthur James Balfour quipped 'I never forgive, but I always forget,' while the American proverb 'Good to forgive, best to forget' emerged only in the mid 20th century.

However, the common phrase 'forgive and forget' can be traced back to Shakespeare's tragedy *King Lear*, albeit inverted. The hiatus between the phrase's origins and its popular usage is explained by the fact that Shakespeare was not revered as the greatest bard of Britain until the nineteenth century, when he was championed by the Romantics. This is precisely when we start seeing variations of his phrase being used.

These days, the expression is used as counsel. However, to borrow and bend another line from Shakespeare, it is advice more honoured in the breach than the observance. People commend it, but few seem convinced of it. As Thomas Szasz put it, 'The stupid neither forgive nor forget; the naïve forgive and forget; the wise forgive but do not forget.'

In *King Lear*, the words are uttered by the eponymous

monarch in Act IV, when he is sick, disorientated and full of regret. To his daughter Cordelia he says, 'If you have poison for me, I will drink it. I know you do not love me . . . you have some cause.' He later continues, 'You must bear with me: Pray you now, forget and forgive: I am old and foolish.'

This recommendation of forgetful forgiveness is a plea from the guilty, not neutral advice to the wronged. Furthermore, it is a plea from someone at the end of life, for whom compassion is most appropriate. Both forgetting and forgiving is therefore an extreme form of leniency, to be granted in exceptional cases, not routinely. This we must remember, before we implore to forget.

Compare and contrast

To err is human; to forgive, divine. *Alexander Pope (1688–1744)*

And we forget because we must / And not because we will. *Matthew Arnold (1822–88)*

Everyone says forgiveness is a lovely idea, until they have something to forgive. *C. S. Lewis (1898–1963)*

9. Practice makes perfect

Mid 16th century

In his book *Outliers*, Malcolm Gladwell claims that 'researchers have settled on what they believe is a magic number for true expertise: 10,000 hours'. Does this mean that science has finally shown exactly how much practice is required to make perfect?

Ten thousand hours is a suspiciously round number, but the neurologist Daniel Levitin claims the same figure comes up in 'study after study'. It was first spotted as significant by the psychologist K. Anders Ericsson, whose research suggested this was the amount of practice required by talented violinists to become elite performers.

Assuming the research is fundamentally sound, what does it really show? No one claims that anyone can become an expert, just as long as they put in the practice. Ericsson's study was based on students who had already been admitted to Berlin's elite Academy of Music. Ten thousand hours may maximize your potential, but no amount of time spent with a needle and thread can turn a sow's ear into a silk purse.

The experimental pop band Sparks captured another limitation of the proverb in their song 'How Do I Get To Carnegie Hall?', to which the legendary answer is, of course, 'Practice'. 'The audience was deafening, I was ready,' sang Russell Mael, but 'Still there is no sign of you.' Even when practice makes you really good, there's no guarantee your accomplishment will be recognized.

In everyday life, we encourage each other with the thought that practice makes perfect, not because we're trying to become true masters, but simply because we want to get better. The 10,000-hour rule in some ways supports common sense, in that it shows even the most talented need to work at it. But the caveats that surround the claim should also make us question just how useful the advice is. How much better we get with rehearsal depends a lot on our natural aptitudes, and there are some things which would take so much time to get good at, we would perhaps be better off focusing our energies elsewhere. If anything less than 10,000 hours won't even ensure we're up there with the best, then unless the practice is itself rewarding, it's not much of an investment.

Compare and contrast

If at first you don't succeed, try, try, try again. *Late 17th century*

A master has never yet fallen from the sky. *German proverb*

It's by forging that you become a blacksmith. *French proverb*

10. Love never fails

1 Corinthians 13:8

At almost every church wedding, in Britain at least, the Bible reading will be chapter 13 of the first of St Paul's letters to the Corinthians. 'Love is patient, love is kind,' writes Paul. 'It always protects, always trusts, always hopes, always perseveres.' It never fails and without it we are nothing.

But although it seems like a perfect match for a wedding, it is not quite what it seems. The clue comes in the King James Bible where the trio of faith, hope and love which ends the chapter becomes the more familiar collocation of faith, hope and charity. The word 'love' is absent throughout.

In fact, the chapter is not about charity or love in the normal, current meanings of those words. It is about *agapē*, one of several ancient Greek words usually translated as love. *Agapē* is often defined as Christian love, although the word obviously predates the New Testament. The romantic love we have more in mind at weddings is *eros,* with perhaps a dash of *philia.*

It seems countless brides and grooms have been victims of a kind of linguistic illusion. But those who know what a*gapē* actually means might find the passage even more enriching.

When Jesus told his followers to love their neighbours, he was talking of *agapē*, not *eros* or *philia.* And, of course, this makes perfect sense. Romantic love is not something we can choose to give. *Agapē,* on the other hand, is voluntary. We can go out and love our neighbours in this sense, even if we don't like them.

At a wedding, this reminder that not all love arises as a spontaneous feeling is extremely valuable. To engage in a lifelong commitment on the presupposition that the love that brought you together will keep you together is naive. Romantic love often does fail. The solemn vows of marriage make sense only on the understanding that the love that binds is at least in part a love that we will to exist, and not just something that springs up of its own accord.

Compare and contrast

Love will find a way. *Early 17th century*

Omnia vincit Amor. (Love conquers all.) *Virgil (70–19 BCE)*

The love that lasts longest is the love that is never returned. *W. Somerset Maugham (1874–1965)*

11. Actions speak louder
than words

17th century

While prime minister, Tony Blair twice postponed judging his own record, once by saying history would do the job for him, and once by saying God would do the same thing. If either could speak, then surely both would reach their verdicts on the basis of his actions, rather than his words. The problem, however, is that actions don't speak English.

Paul Foot, for example, heard a 'shameful British involvement in the invasion and occupation of Iraq' and the pursuit of 'Tory policies every bit as ardently as the Tories would have done'. Polly Toynbee and David Walker, on the other hand, believed the actions of Blair's government created a Britain which was 'richer, fairer, healthier, safer and better-educated'. Do you hear something quite different?

It is because actions do not speak unambiguously that we are in a strange position where both supporters and detractors of governments make their cases by insisting we must not believe what they say in public. Don't listen to what they say about choice and opportunity, say the knockers, look at their record on tax increases, bureaucracy and centralization. Don't listen to what they say to appease the tabloid press, say supporters, look at their record on redistribution of wealth and investment in public services.

Actions are speaking all right, but in a cacophony of conflicting voices.

Interpreting the meaning of actions is fraught with difficulty. Consider how people can only do what is possible for them at the time, and how in politics, the room for manoeuvre can be very small. For example, if America hadn't been hell-bent on invading Iraq according to its own timetable, would Blair have acted otherwise, and thus sent out a different message? It's a tough question, but without an answer it is impossible to know exactly what the actions he actually did take meant.

None of this is to deny that actions do indeed speak louder than words. It's just that to understand them, you need to be a skilled interpreter.

Compare and contrast

Example is better than precept. *Early 15th century*

A worker is known by his work. *French proverb*

The poor writer blames his pen. *Spanish proverb*

12. That which does not kill me makes me stronger

Friedrich Nietzsche (1844–1900)

An advocate of the fledgling practice of philosophical counselling was once asked what advice he would give a parent whose children were refusing to do their bit to keep the home clean and tidy. He suggested that the parent remind the feckless youths of Nietzsche's maxim, 'That which does not kill me makes me stronger.'

One quick-witted and extremely rude reply a kid could give, if proffered this advice, is 'Why don't you just fuck off? After all, it won't kill you, so it will make you stronger.' Although the politeness of the response is questionable, its logic is impeccable.

To think that literally everything that does not kill us makes us stronger is to interpret Nietzsche in an appallingly simple-minded, literal way. As a mere matter of fact, it is plainly false. Misfortune can leave people considerably emaciated, emotionally and physically. If that weren't the case, then by the time we retired we would all be indestructible powerhouses.

Nietzsche's aphorism is not a statement of fact but a resolution: I will try to ensure that every experience I go through, no matter how bad, will be turned to my ultimate advantage. If I make a mistake, I will try to learn from it. If I survive an ordeal, I will use the knowledge that I did pull through to strengthen me in times of future hardship.

That's why it's no use simply quoting Nietzsche to someone having a hard time and expecting it to console them. There is absolutely no inevitability that they will emerge from their ordeal stronger than at the start. It takes willpower, if not a Nietzschean 'will to power', to turn adversity to advantage. To believe that hard times naturally empower us couldn't get Nietzsche more wrong, since his point is precisely that it is all down to us how we deal with difficulty. That which does not kill you may well make you weaker, if you let it.

Compare and contrast

What won't kill you, will feed you. *Italian proverb*

What does not kill, fattens. *Spanish proverb*

Our torments also may in length of time / Become our elements. *John Milton (1608–74)*

13. The exception proves the rule

Late 17th century

Sometimes a good idea can be lost between the sloppy, who make it too vague to be useful, and the pedantic, who demand it be so specific as to be irrelevant.

In this case, the sloppy are the majority who take 'the exception proves the rule' to mean 'every rule has an exception' and use it to justify diverging from a moral norm ('but stealing is wrong!'), or a factual one ('no one ever got rich betting on horses'). In each case, someone who is convinced that the rule need not apply to them will blather about exceptions.

But whether a rule has exceptions depends on the rule. Laws of physics don't – at least not in any situation medium-sized objects like ourselves are going to find ourselves in. The rule 'don't steal' may have exceptions, but pointing out this fact doesn't justify my particular act of stealing unless I go on to explain why it is exceptional.

Pedants just dismiss this common usage as degenerate. The 'prove' of the phrase actually comes from the old French *prover*, in turn from the Latin *probare*, meaning to test. Exceptions do not simply show rules exist, they test them so that we may revise them to fit observations they currently don't.

This is fair enough, but it is not much use in everyday

speech. Fortunately, however, there is a way of understanding the phrase which is both sensible and true to its original 17th-century usage. In order to notice that something is an exception to a rule, we have to recognize that there is a rule in the first place. Exceptions, therefore, highlight both their own difference and what is ordinarily the case. There is no bogus justification here or pedantic appeal to etymology: just a pithy way of capturing an everyday truth.

Incidentally, one could ask, does 'every rule has an exception' have an exception? If it does not, then it is false. But if it does, then there is at least one rule which does not have an exception, namely that 'every rule has an exception'. Hence the principle is self-defeating, because if it's true it's false.

Compare and contrast

Science has no enemy but the ignorant. *Mid 16th century*

One swallow does not make a summer. *Mid 16th century*

How seldom is it that theories stand the wear and tear of practice! *Anthony Trollope (1815–82)*

14. All happy families resemble one another, but each unhappy family is unhappy in its own way

Leo Tolstoy (1828–1910)

When children miss out on something they evidently crave, they often say, 'I didn't want it anyway.' Young habits die hard. Happiness is almost universally desired, though not at any price. However, few achieve it more than fleetingly, and even when we do, it is fragile. Rather than live with the imperfection of life, however, it is tempting to say, 'I didn't want it anyway.' Happy people, we tell ourselves, are stupid, boring or both.

It's not that we often explicitly articulate such a belief. But the idea that misery is somehow a marker of depth is often implicit in what we say and do. Tolstoy betrayed this prejudice in his comment about happy families. The falsity of his claim is made evident by its plausible inversion. Unhappy families are characterized by either conflict and tension, or an emotional sterility beneath a surface calm. Often common to both types is an absence of love. Happy families, however, come in many sorts. Take the marital relationship first. Some spouses are soulmates, others very independent. Some remain sexually passionate, others emotionally warm and some function happily with little intimacy at all. Some are steadfastly faithful, while others tolerate occasional – or even ongoing –

infidelity. Add in the various ways parents relate to their children and you have enormous variety.

What is actually most likely is that happy and unhappy families are equally diverse. So why the prevalence of the idea that happy ones are more alike? Perhaps it is the intolerability of the thought that life is unfair. If other people are happier than ourselves, justice demands that they pay some price for it, and being shallow or boring would fit that bill. Likewise, life may be miserable for us, but at least we're men and women of substance.

But as John Stuart Mill put it, even if it is true that 'It is better to be a human being dissatisfied than a pig satisfied,' not all the content are hogs, and we are not ennobled by our dissatisfaction, but harmed by it.

Compare and contrast

The joys of parents are secret, and so are their griefs and fears. *Francis Bacon (1561–1626)*

Few misfortunes can befall a boy which bring worse consequences than to have a really affectionate mother. *W. Somerset Maugham (1874–1965)*

They fuck you up, your mum and dad. *Philip Larkin (1922–85)*

15. No pain, no gain

Late 16th century

The Law of Contrasts is what I call the folk wisdom which states that, in order to appreciate a thing, it is necessary to experience its contrary. Its weak version merely requires some experience of the negative at some point. For example, you can know what love means only if your heart has been broken. The strong version insists on some ongoing acquaintance with the dark side, making unremitting happiness a human impossibility.

Although it is true that people do generally seem to need reminders of the bad to cherish the good, it is not an iron-clad law that they must. It's possible to cherish what you've got before it's gone, but it can be difficult. In many ways it is more comforting to believe that the bad is a necessary complement to the good. Then we can tell ourselves we didn't waste the opportunity of good times, it was just that we somehow weren't able to make the most of them.

Take work, for example. In many countries, those lucky enough to have jobs pay the hefty price of having little time left for the things they really enjoy. It would be easy to reassure ourselves that we need all this work to make us appreciate the days off when they come, rather than face the possibility that our lives are out of balance.

In *Henry IV*, Part One, Shakespeare says something more

circumspect: 'If all the year were playing holidays; To sport would be as tedious as to work.' That is not to say longer ones wouldn't be very nice indeed. What's more, 'sport' is not the only enjoyable activity we would do more of if we had time. His line would not have rung true had it been, 'If all the year were reading, painting and doing the garden, that would be as tedious as to work.'

Life does indeed benefit from a certain contrast of light and shade. But there is all the difference in the world between living under a parasol or in the gloom of a Scandinavian winter.

Compare and contrast

There is no honey without gall. *Spanish proverb*

A squirrel who eats dried chapattis would not know the taste of sugar. *Indian proverb*

Adversity does best discover virtue. *Francis Bacon (1561–1626)*

16. If you can't stand the heat, get out of the kitchen

Major General Harry Vaughan (1888–1964)

Trust a man to come up with such a macho, simplistic solution to a problem. Sweat it out or shut up is a stark challenge, but it ignores other more agreeable solutions. Why not install air-conditioning or just open a window? Why tolerate the temperature when it is adjustable?

The metaphor should strike a chord with anyone concerned about women's rights in the workplace. So often, professions have their ways of operating, and newcomers are told what they can do if they don't like them. This conveniently glosses over the fact that things needn't be this way at all, and they are as they are only because the men who have run the show for centuries like them that way. Late-night sittings at the House of Commons, for example, are not a requirement of a democratic legislature, but they do make the atmosphere of parliament more like that of a gentleman's drinking club.

A gentler, but no less stifling, kind of heat is produced by the rituals and traditions of Oxford and Cambridge. To have to wear ridiculous gowns on various stipulated occasions hardly seems to serve the purpose of educating the country's finest minds. Indeed, it looks more like a means of perpetuating idiocy. Nevertheless, this and countless other little points of etiquette together can have the effect of making those with humbler origins feel that this is one kitchen in which they shouldn't be attempting to cook.

The saying is certainly true when applied literally: being a chef is bloody hard work, and if you're at all inclined to laziness, you really are better doing the eating rather than the cooking. And there are many other spheres of life where things are inevitably tough and you just have to accept it or move on. The saying was actually immortalized when someone gave in to its challenge rather than issued it: Harry Truman quoted it in 1952 to explain why he was retiring.

But on countless other occasions the temperature is being kept artificially high, and ventilation, rather than capitulation, is the solution you should demand.

Compare and contrast

You cannot make an omelette without breaking eggs. *Mid 19th century*

Fleas jump on a sickly dog. *Spanish proverb*

If you say A, you have to say B as well. *German proverb*

17. Night brings counsel

Late 16th century

It is in some ways strange that one of the most common pieces of advice for people facing a hard decision is that we enter a state in which we not only do nothing but also don't even know we're not doing it. So how exactly does a good night's sleep contribute to our decision-making, other than helping us to delay it? There are, of course, good reasons for not rushing into a decision if you don't have to, but there is also an increasing amount of research that suggests that sleep itself, not just the passage of time, can move our thinking forward, in at least two ways.

The first concerns formal problem-solving. For example, in an experiment, subjects were given a number of tasks, such as logic puzzles which require you to work out what comes next in the sequence. They were then tested again, later the same day. Those who slept in the interval regularly performed better than those who didn't. Functional MRI scans suggest that the reason for this is that the brain 'rehearses' in sleep precisely those brain patterns involved in problems that have been occupying us while awake.

Another way sleep changes thought, however, is of more questionable value. Most memories fade with time, whether we sleep or not. But there is one exception: our memories of emotionally evocative people, places or events actually seem to *improve* after a night's sleep.[2]

Whether this is a help or hindrance depends. If your feelings about something are an important factor in what decision you should make, then it may indeed help for less affecting factors to slip from your mind and the more affecting ones to move centre-stage. But on many occasions, such rejigging might cloud your judgement. Sleep might help you forget some important, but emotionally neutral factors and focus more on less important, perhaps changeable, factors with negative emotional connotations. For instance, the repaintable walls of a house which remind you of a much hated place may cloud out the many advantages of a prospective new home.

Sleeping on it, then, probably does shed new light on a problem, but that does not mean we should always take the advice the night brings.

Compare and contrast

If time comes, advice comes. *German proverb*

The bad of the morning, becomes worse by the night. *Greek proverb*

The evening rage – put it away for the morning. *Italian proverb*

18. I may disagree with what you have to say, but I shall defend to the death your right to say it

Voltaire (1694–1778)

A newspaper publishes false allegations which ruin someone's career. A group of men calls 'nigger' across the street to a lone black man. A woman in a male-dominated office faces a constant trickle of sexist language from her colleagues. Was Voltaire seriously suggesting that though we can disagree with what was said in each case, each speaker had a perfect right to say it?

Hopefully not. The principle of free speech which Voltaire so memorably championed certainly applies to the arena of civilized discussion. No opinion is so vile that it should not be discussed openly and rejected on the basis of vigorous debate, not censorship. The open society needs to ensure there is room for all opinions to be heard and discussed.

Problems arise, however, when we fail to see that outside salons and debating chambers, our words are not just audible expressions of thought but acts with consequences. The journalist isn't merely expressing an opinion, she is actually harming a person's life. The racist creates fear and incites violence. The sexist buttresses unequal practices in the workplace.

As the philosopher J. L. Austin put it, we don't just utter words – we *do things with them*. Constant verbal mockery can *make* a person's life a misery; spreading falsehoods can *turn* others against them. Sexist language in the workplace or racist abuse in the street are not contributions to debate, but attacks on the rights of others, deliberate or otherwise. What is going on in such cases is more than just speech, which is why appeals to freedom of speech are not enough to justify permitting language that causes harm.

The complication is that words are always to some extent acts as well as utterances. Hence the frequent complaint that merely giving prejudiced views a hearing legitimatizes them. It is a complication we must live with. The boundaries of acceptable free speech cannot be drawn precisely and will always be disputed, hopefully by rational debate.

Compare and contrast

Hard words break no bones. *Late 17th century*

Every man has a right to utter what he thinks truth, and every other man has a right to knock him down for it. *Samuel Johnson (1709–84)*

Freedom is the freedom to say that two plus two make four. *George Orwell (1903–50)*

19. Penny wise and pound foolish

Early 17th century

Take care of the pence and the pounds will take care of themselves

Mid 18th century

The proverbial battle between pounds and pence took a vital turn between the early 17th and mid 18th century. Pounds began this conflict in the ascendancy, as people who took too much care of their small change were mocked for missing the bigger financial picture. But after the English Civil War, the Great Fire and plagues of London, and the beginning of Imperial conquest, suddenly pennies were back in vogue as the main unit of currency we should worry about.

Such a dubious narrative is never going to appear in any history books, not least because the English language's two most famous sayings about pounds and pence are not contradictory but complementary.

One is penny wise and pound foolish when one spends less than what is needed to do the job properly with an eye to making a saving. Such false economies do not put major pieces of expenditure in the greater and longer-term context. Sometimes you need to spend big to save big.

On the other hand, most of our spending is actually on small things. Here, one is unlikely to be seduced by potentially large savings, but one needs to avoid the thinking behind the paradox of the heap. This ancient puzzle considers what would happen if you thought that removing a single grain of sand from a heap can never stop it being a heap. One by one you could remove each grain and be left with just one, which you would then be committed to saying was still a heap. In a similar way, make enough small savings and you can end up with a big one.

The two proverbs are thus pieces of the same jigsaw. Not being wasteful with small things, not only money, can have a significant cumulative effect. But that is not the same as refusing to pay enough to get quality with major purchases. Proper thrift is not always about paying as little as possible. Indeed, one way to make sure you do have the pounds when they are needed is to watch the pennies when they aren't.

Compare and contrast

Wilful waste makes woeful want. *Early 18th century*

Bean by bean, the sack gets full. *Greek proverb*

Add up your pennies, and buy a hen. *Polish proverb*

20. A journey of a thousand miles begins with a single step

Lao Tzu (c.604–531 BCE)

'Procrastination is the thief of time,' wrote the poet Edward Young. Indeed, the thief is so prolific that the aeons he has stashed away would surely stretch back to the Triassic. It's easy pickings. Instead of guarding precious time, we leave piles of it here and there, as though there were an endless supply of the stuff.

One reason we do this is because we suffer from temporal myopia. The further time stretches out, the blurrier it seems. When what is far off seems so indistinct, it is easy to think that it is not really there at all. When it finally comes round, then, we find ourselves completely unprepared.

Working for future goals is also hampered by the despair induced by scale. Building a work of years out of minutes and seconds can seem like trying to dig a tunnel with a teaspoon. Positive action requires motivation, and nothing is more demotivating than the thought that our resources are not enough for the job at hand.

The thought that the journey of a thousand miles begins with a single step is therefore often an extremely helpful one. It is a reminder that all great endeavours can be broken down into doable component pieces.

The danger, however, is that this reassurance can provide

false comfort. For whether the journey is completed or not depends not only on the direction of travel, but also the velocity. It is easy to kid yourself that small steps in the right direction are enough and that you need to move at your own pace, when, actually, you're just not doing enough. Doing something 'in your own time' is all well and good, just as long as you have enough of it.

What we need to remember is that although the journey of a thousand miles begins with a single step, it is completed only when you take the remaining 5,279 of them, one at a time. So don't panic if at your back you always hear Time's wing'd chariot hurrying near. Just make sure you're going fast enough that it doesn't overtake you.

Compare and contrast

Little strokes fell great oaks. *Early 15th century*

Slow and steady wins the race. *Mid 18th century*

What's well begun is half done. *Italian proverb*

21. Make hay while the sun shines

Mid 16th century

An old hermit who has devoted her life to learning is granted one wish. 'All my life,' she tells her supernatural benefactor, 'I have struggled to share whatever wisdom I have learned. I failed, and that is why I have retreated from the world. If you could ensure my thoughts are set down, printed and widely read across the land, you will have saved me from my greatest disappointment.'

The wish is granted. To her surprise, the woman lives many years more and decides to travel to see the effect her teachings have had. She is shocked to find that everyone has indeed read her work, but they seem to believe the opposite of what she intended. She then realizes her mistake: it is one thing for people to know what you have said, another for them to have understood it.

That such total misunderstanding is possible is shown by the way in which many people now take the advice to make hay while the sun shines. They rightly understand the injunction to make the most of favourable conditions while they last. But how do they do this? By enjoying themselves, savouring the moment, living for today. Have fun now, for tomorrow it may rain.

This is the exact opposite of what the proverb originally advised. Making hay is all about hard work today to prepare for difficult times ahead. We are to sweat and toil under the shining sun, not play in it. If we don't do that, we won't be able to make up for it when conditions are much worse.

However, this distortion is not entirely bad. Both original and inverted forms of the saying capture part of the truth, but only together do they grasp all of it. The good life requires a balance between enjoying the good times while they last and preparing for bad times before they come. Neither the person who always plays in the fields nor the one who only works in them has her priorities quite straight. We must live for today as well as, not instead of, for tomorrow.

Compare and contrast

Strike while the iron is hot. *Late 14th century*

Time and tide wait for no man. *Late 14th century*

No time like the present. *Mid 16th century*

22. First do no harm

Galen (129–200)

The maxim that doctors have followed for millennia is also one that seems apt for individuals and governments. The actor Paul Eddington, for example, once said in an interview that he hoped his epitaph could truthfully say 'He did very little harm.' Keeping the nasty side of human nature at bay is a real moral achievement; saintliness can come later.

But how does one avoid doing harm? It would be absurd to say that we should simply never do anything if some harm might result. Thankfully, that is not the maxim doctors follow. From their willingness to scar your flesh in order to fix your heart, to the decision to amputate a foot to save the leg, physicians often cause some harm as a means to a higher end.

To avoid absurdity we have to understand the rule as meaning that we should always leave things no worse than they would otherwise have been. But that doesn't do the work that many hope 'first do no harm' should. For instance, many invoke the principle as a reason not to go to war. The one thing we know happens when wars start is that people die. First do no harm, so first don't fight.

But as we've seen, all the principle can sensibly mean is that no war should leave things worse than they would otherwise have been. With the benefit of hindsight, many wars do not seem to have fulfilled this condition. But when decisions to fight are made, it is usually the case that many sensible people see good reasons to believe that keeping the troops at home may condemn more people to a worse fate in the long run. In such cases, who is really advocating the course of least harm?

The same kind of uncertainty affects any area of life where action could make things worse, which is more or less everywhere. To do no harm is a worthy aspiration. But it is far from easy to know how we must act to live up to it.

Compare and contrast

The more you stir it the worse it stinks. *Mid 16th century*

If you play with fire you get burnt. *Late 19th century*

A spark can start a fire that burns the entire prairie. *Chinese proverb*

23. Speech is silver, but silence is golden

Mid 19th century

Some sayings are so open and ambiguous they can mean more or less whatever you want them to mean. 'Silence is golden' has become like this. It can be uttered by those advocating the virtues of a monastic life, parents trying to shut their children up, miscreants seeking to cover up their misdeeds, the fearful worried not to rock the boat, and many more.

Nevertheless, its original formulation does point to two specific subtleties which are often missed nowadays. First, the phrase emerged at a time when etiquette and good manners had been elevated to virtues in their own right rather than means to the end of civility. It was originally used to encourage discretion, and so was in its essence about the promotion of supposedly benign deceit. Discretion may sometimes be the better part of valour, but it is worth remembering that the value placed on silence in such contexts reflects wider social norms which we may no longer agree with.

Second, the metaphors of silver and gold suggest not just variations in intrinsic value but in regularity of use. Silver cutlery, for example, is used more often than a gold terrine. Silence being golden, it is not only more precious but should perhaps be used more sparingly. Maybe monks should seek another expression.

What both these points reinforce is that silence comes in many forms. The silence of two lovers caught deep in each other's gaze is quite different from that of the long married couple, facing each other across a restaurant table with nothing to say.

Silence can be habitual, tactical, repressive, attentive, inattentive, thoughtful, absent-minded, welcomed, dreaded. Some of these silences are better compared to base metals than gold. Think of the vile contexts in which children have been told 'This is our little secret – don't tell anyone.'

Perhaps that is why Francis Bacon said 'Silence is the virtue of fools.' To value silence for its own sake is to misunderstand how its supreme value lies in its skilful use, not in its unthinking pursuit and devotion.

Compare and contrast

A shut mouth catches no flies. *Late 16th century*

It is a great thing to know the season for speech and the season for silence. *Seneca (4 BCE–65AD)*

Whereof one cannot speak, thereof one must be silent. *Ludwig Wittgenstein (1889–1951)*

24. Reading is to the mind as exercise is to the body

Sir Richard Steele (1672–1729)

If reading is a workout for the mind, then Britain must be buzzing with intellectual energy. Train stations, for example, have shops packed with enough words to keep even the most muscular brain engaged for weeks. Indeed, the carriages are full of people exercising their intellects the full length of their journeys.

Yet somehow, the fact that millions daily devour thousands of words from celebrity magazines, tabloid newspapers and airport novels does not inspire the hope that the average cerebrum is in excellent health. It's not just *that* you read, it's *what* you read that counts.

There are some good reasons why reading is often thought to be a good thing regardless of what is being read. Enid Blyton used to be defended against her critics on the grounds that reading was a good habit to instil in children, and many who grew to love books through her work would progress to more challenging material later. But while that may be true, the hope that adults who read only the likes of *Heat* and *Hello!* will one day graduate to the *Economist* is surely misplaced.

Reading has also been highly prized because it is a basic skill without which it is very hard to get on in life. But while that is a good reason to strive for 100 per cent literacy, it does not even begin to prove the point that reading will inevitably provide training for the mind.

Yet the feeling that reading is an intrinsically intellectual activity persists. Worse, books are given a special reverence that other forms of the written word are not. People lament the hours children spend on computers, but a lot of that time is spent reading.

Reading feeds the mind as food does the body. Which means that it can do so well or badly, depending on whether what you ingest is nourishing or junk.

Compare and contrast

A book is like a garden carried in the pocket. *American proverb, mid 20th century*

A library is a repository of medicine for the mind. *Greek proverb*

People say that life is the thing, but I prefer reading. *Logan Pearsall Smith (1865–1946)*

25. Practise what you preach

Late 14th century

Righteous indignation is rarely more justified than when it is a response to gross hypocrisy. However, the rule that people should indeed practise what they preach is not entirely without exception, and nor does it have all the implications sometimes attributed to it.

One legitimate reason not to practise what you preach is the division of labour. Those giving orders can be fully justified in not doing what they instruct others to do, if it would prevent them from doing their own jobs effectively. This has its counterpart in moral life. For example, it is not hypocritical for a priest who has taken a vow of celibacy to encourage his flock to wed and multiply, for in his view and that of his church, the roles of priest and husband are incompatible. Nor should those who encourage charitable works necessarily undertake them themselves, if their talents, inclinations or circumstances are not up to the job. For instance, there are many reasons to spurn charity 'chuggers' who accost you in the street, but the fact that they may not have signed the kind of direct debit mandate they are trying to get your signature on is not one of them: maybe they just can't afford one.

Even if someone should practise what they preach but fails to do so, that doesn't mean that their advice is automatically invalid. What is preached can be a noble aspiration that few are able to follow to the letter. The injunction to love thy neighbour is one people consistently fail to honour, yet many maintain it is worth trying.

Good advice which others are able to follow can also come from people too weak or foolish to heed it themselves. That's why bad parents can be good child psychologists, inefficient managers good management consultants, and poor historians good history teachers. As the philosopher Ted Honderich wrote, '"Do as I say, not as I have done," whatever it tells you of the sayer, may be exactly the right instruction.'

Compare and contrast

Fine words butter no parsnips. *Mid 17th century*

Teacher who taught, but did not keep your books. *Greek saying*

Cobblers have the worst shoes. *French proverb*

26. Greater love hath no man than this, that a man lay down his life for his friends

John 15:13

It takes some effort to see the Bible as the literal word of God without doubting the intelligence of our creator. Take, for example, John 15, in which Jesus reportedly said, 'You are my friends if you do what I command.' That's a definition of friendship not usually given outside the primary school playground. The faithful, however, simply accept that Jesus is a friend like no other, and has his own rules.

More troubling is the idea that the greatest act of love is to lay down your life for your friends. Elsewhere in the Good Book, a certain Samaritan is praised for kindness to a complete stranger. This doesn't contradict John, because although it may be the highest *virtue* to help someone you don't even know, the highest *love* could only be for someone you know.

Nevertheless, the contrast with the Samaritan is still suggestive. The power of the parable is that it undermines the kind of sectarian, parochial thinking that fuels conflict between peoples. This is indeed one of Jesus' most progressive messages. He speaks of a universalism in which you strive to love all your neighbours as yourself, and not just those who are bound to you by family, culture or religion.

To praise the love of friends as the greatest kind chafes

against this message, even if it doesn't plain contradict it. 'My friends, right or wrong' is as morally reprehensible as 'my country, right or wrong' or 'my people, right or wrong'. You should lay down you life for your friends, country or people only if you are doing so in a good cause: kinship is not enough. Those who would die to protect their would-be suicide-bombing friends, for example, would surely be reproached, not praised, by Christ.

The conclusion therefore seems inescapable: If John is a true witness, then either the greatest love can sometimes be misplaced, or Jesus was plain wrong.

Compare and contrast

A friend in need is a friend indeed. *Mid 11th century*

A man, Sir, should keep his friendship in constant repair. *Samuel Johnson (1709–84)*

Martyrdom . . . the only way in which a man can become famous without ability. *George Bernard Shaw (1856–1950)*

27. Que será, será

Ray Evans (1915–2007)

In 1956, Doris Day first sang a song whose title would become one of the most familiar sayings in English. Not in Spanish though, where it is actually meaningless. It's not the only English phrase of bastardized Spanish origin, though, so as we say, and they don't, *no problemo.*

The exact wording may have been a twentieth-century invention, but the basic sentiment recurs at almost all times, in almost every culture. There is, however, one important variation in how it is expressed or understood, reflected in the 14th-century British version, 'What must be, must be.'

The difference between the two versions is critical. If you say, 'What must be, must be,' it is reasonable to ask what *must be* and what *could be different.* If you say, 'What will be, will be,' then that is by definition true, but it doesn't tell you how what will be will actually come to be. Is it inevitable, or can we do something to change it?

In practice, the wording makes little difference because all versions of the phrase tend to be uttered as statements of resignation. But is such fatalism justified?

There are philosophical arguments that lead us to a determinist world view in which there is only one possible future. But this makes little or no practical difference to how we live. In such a universe, what we decide and do still causes things to happen, it's just that at some deep level those choices and actions were inevitable.

A stronger fatalism says that what will happen will happen irrespective of what we do. But this seems plain false. No outside forces alter the course of nature, making sure that only one set of outcomes results.

The only time it is useful to accept that the future is fixed is when a chain of events is too far advanced for us to alter it. When all that can be done, has been done, then whatever will be, will be. But until that point, the future may not be ours to see, but it may yet be ours to change.

Compare and contrast

He who is born to be a mule, from heaven will fall his harness. *Spanish proverb*

What isn't yet can still become. *German proverb*

Every bullet has its billet. *William III (1650–1702)*

28. Plus ça change, plus c'est la même chose

Alphonse Karr (1808–90)

People often use the abbreviated version of the French phrase, '*plus ça change, plus c'est la même chose*', and the 16th-century variant of Ecclesiastes, 'there is nothing new under the sun', as though they were interchangeable. Look at each in its own right, however, and subtle but important differences emerge. And in this instance, French writer Alphonse Karr gets the better of biblical authority. To say nothing is new is only half right.

In the opening verses of Ecclesiastes, the theme is of vanity. We are reminded that all our labours leave the world as it is. 'One generation passeth away, and another generation cometh: but the earth abideth for ever.'

The same idea recurs in Shelley's 'Ozymandias', where a traveller recalls coming across the ruins of a statue, the plinth of which bore the inscription, 'My name is Ozymandias, King of Kings, Look on my Works, ye Mighty, and despair!'

The key message here is that human beings come and go, while things greater than ourselves, such as time and the earth, abide unaffected by our brief appearance.

In Ecclesiastes, the idea that nothing is new is really a kind of poetic overstatement of the idea that all that is, has been and will be is already within the horizon of the eye of eternity.

Plus ça change, on the other hand, really is about change from the human point of view. The central idea here is not that it is hubris to think we can leave a mark on the universe, but that what is continuous in culture is more fundamental than what changes. It is not a simple lament that things never change, but an expression of how there is continuity in change. Both parts of the phrase – the more things change and the more they stay the same – are needed for it to make real sense. There are, after all, new things under the sun. It's just that basic facts about human nature and culture are not among their number.

Compare and contrast

The leopard does not change his spots. *Mid 16th century*

It's the same dog with a different collar. *Spanish saying*

There is nothing permanent except change. *Heraclitus (c. 535–475 BCE)*

29. There are three kinds of lies: lies, damned lies and statistics

Benjamin Disraeli, attributed (1804–81)

Given that trust is so important in politics, it is odd that all parties back themselves up with facts and figures which people don't trust at all. The public is sceptical of statistics because numbers are thrown about on both sides to support different conclusions. One side cites the number of children leaving primary school unable to write properly, while the other trumpets record levels of literacy and numeracy. The opposition point to high levels of violent crime, while the government claims to have cut it. People complain of long hospital waiting lists, while others say they're shorter than ever.

Yet statisticians have every right to be peeved at Disraeli's withering dismissal of the fruits of their labours. The only statistics that lie are false ones, which makes them no different from any other kind of putative fact. The competing statistics cited by politicians are usually true and do not contradict one another. It's what they mean which is disputable.

In order to understand properly what statistics mean you have to look behind the headlines to how they were collected and what precisely they measure. If we can't be bothered to do this, it is our own fault if we are fooled by the politicians who obviously select the numbers that make their own position look stronger and then present them in the most self-serving way. The problem is not that the figures they use are false, it is that they may not actually back up the point that the politician is trying to make with them.

The idea that you can prove anything with statistics is just false. The lies that surround statistics are to be found in what people claim they show, not in the numbers themselves. Don't blame the statisticians when you're fooled by the gloss others put on their results.

Compare and contrast

You might prove anything by figures. *Thomas Carlyle (1795–1881)*

If you want to inspire confidence, give plenty of statistics. *Lewis Carroll (1832–98)*

He uses statistics as a drunken man uses lampposts – for support rather than for illumination. *Herbert Asquith (1852–1928)*

30. Time will tell

Mid 16th century

When asked what he thought about the French Revolution, 160 years on, China's communist premier Zhou Enlai famously replied, 'It is too soon to say.' It's an extreme example of a common idea: that the truth about things often emerges only slowly.

Since the proverb counsels against rushing, it would be apt not to rush to jump to conclusions about what precisely it means. There are at least two ways of getting it wrong.

One is suggested by an Italian variant, *Se son rose, fioriranno*: if they're roses, they'll bloom. But even hardy plants like roses won't bloom if they are neglected. Often, more than time is needed if something is to show its full potential. If you could be a great musician, for example, time is mute about what you could have achieved if you decide not to bother practising. The proverb needs to be purged of any fatalistic overtones if it is to ring true.

Roses of another kind point to the second way the saying can be got wrong. We often think that we will be able to judge whether something in our recent past is good or bad only once enough time has elapsed to give us some distance from it. Again, this might be true, but only if we are careful to remove rose-tinted spectacles. Time tells, but it also heals, and it often does this by helping us to forget. Everyday experience and psychological research agree that we are often very bad at recalling the past impartially, and that we tend to construct narratives that suit ourselves. History may be written by the winners, but even losers find ways to make their defeat less ignominious.

When we look back and ask whether we did the right thing, finding an answer, even a critical one, enables us to come to terms with what has happened. But sometimes this clarity is imposed by hindsight rather than revealed by time, and sometimes it distorts rather than captures what really happened.

Compare and contrast

Time is a great healer. *Late 14th century*

Who shall live shall see. *Spanish proverb*

Hindsight is always 20/20. *Billy Wilder (1906–2002)*

31. All the world's a stage

William Shakespeare (1564–1616)

Theatre is the source of numerous fruitful metaphors for human life. Karl Marx added to Hegel's remark about history repeating itself, saying that it did so 'the first time as tragedy, the second as farce'. Horace Walpole described the world as 'a comedy to those that think, a tragedy to those who feel'. The sociologist Irving Goffman unpacked the metaphor at book length in his seminal *The Presentation of Self in Everyday Life*, describing the extent to which we routinely play roles.

Many spontaneously come to something like the same conclusion at certain moments in their lives, when the disjunction between who they feel they really are and how they have to be on a regular basis becomes too stark. There is a powerful ring of truth in the image of putting on a mask in order to go to work, fit in socially, or even fulfil the role your family has come to expect of you.

Such ways of thinking, however, presuppose that there is a distinction between character and player. But what if all the world's a stage? If we are always performing, don't we simply become our performance? A mask that has nothing behind it or is never taken off is not a mask at all, but a face.

In Jaques's soliloquy in Act II of *As You Like It*, the idea that 'all the men and women' are 'merely players' is clearly not taken to mean that we go through life hiding our true natures. Rather the seven ages of man which comprise the 'acts' of life describe how we really are at each stage, not how we simply pretend to be.

This is closer to the sense of role-playing that Goffman described. It is too simplistic to think that we go through life pretending to be people we are not. When pretence becomes the norm, it is no longer pretence at all. That's why we should choose our roles carefully, because when we inhabit them deeply, we become the characters we play.

Compare and contrast

Faces we see, hearts we can't know. *Spanish proverb*

There are no second acts in American lives. *F. Scott Fitzgerald (1896–1940)*

Life is a cabaret. *Fred Ebb (1933–2004)*

32. Great oaks from little acorns grow

Late 14th century

The advance of science can lead to the retreat of folk wisdom. Metaphors can metamorphosize into quasi-scientific laws in which neither the science nor the insight survives.

Take the example of oaks and acorns. It's a pretty good saying, as long as you remember that for every oak there are thousands of acorns that rot and die. However, there is now a more modern way of saying that small causes can have big effects: the fluttering of a butterfly's wings can set off a tornado on the other side of the world.

The butterfly effect is the most well-known aspect of chaos theory, which describes the way in which very small changes in initial conditions can lead to very large differences in eventual outcomes. But despite superficial similarities, this is very different from the truths expressed in the acorns and oaks saying. Whereas the growth of trees from seeds is a replicable and predictable, if fragile, process, the butterfly effect is unpredictable and uncontrollable.

The difference can be captured in the ambiguity of the phrase 'you never know'. In some contexts it means, why not have a go? You may succeed, you may not, but you won't know until you try. This is the 'never know' of the small acorn. In contrast, the 'never know' of the butterfly is that you have no idea what unforeseen consequences your actions might have.

Does this mean that the acorns encourage, whereas the butterfly discourages? Since you never know what might happen, should we completely give up on trying to control the future? Not at all. Nothing in chaos theory tells us that the existence of unpredictable distant effects is a reason not to do things that have predictable immediate ones. Turning on a kettle may trigger a storm a hundred miles away, but it probably won't and it definitely will boil the water in it. When it comes to ordinary life, acorns and oaks are usually more instructive than butterflies and tornados.

Compare and contrast

It often takes little force to move great masses. *Icelandic proverb*

A thorn stings even if it's small. *Greek proverb*

Drop after drop, there will be a sea. *Polish proverb*

33. The only certainty is that nothing is certain

Pliny the Elder (23–79)

The economist J. K. Galbraith called the last 200 years 'the age of uncertainty'. Social and intellectual upheavals such as the Industrial Revolution, the ideas of Marx, Darwin and Freud shook centuries-old assumptions. For many, this new era has been troubling, but for others the certainty of uncertainty has become a kind of comfort. Why worry about getting it right when there is no sure measure of what is right and wrong in the first place? Why not retreat to a pluralism of different subjective viewpoints, each as valid as another?

Pliny points the way to some answers. His comment on certainty actually came in the context of a chapter in his *Natural History* about God. 'I consider it . . . an indication of human weakness to inquire into the figure and form of God,' he wrote. It was in these areas that he thought nothing was certain. In many other more empirical matters, his views were not so circumspect. For instance, of tortoises he wrote, 'The shavings of the surface of the shell, administered in drink, act as an antaphrodisiac: a thing that is the more surprising, from the fact that a powder prepared from the whole of the shell has the reputation of being a strong aphrodisiac.'[3]

Even if we accept the more extreme claim that absolutely nothing is certain, we can still do better than permissive shoulder-shrugging. When it comes to God, for example, what we think is true makes a real difference to how we live. If we can't have certainty, we have to decide on the basis of the balance of probability. Nor need that balance be delicate: one can think it very probable that God does or doesn't exist without being entirely certain.

In many other matters, absence of certainty is little more than technical. The fact that eating well is not certain to keep you healthy, and that jumping off a tall building won't inevitably kill you, are not reasons for becoming dietary and leaping agnostics. All beliefs are uncertain, but some are more uncertain than others.

Compare and contrast

Nothing is certain but death and taxes. *Early 18th century*

Nothing is certain but the unforeseen. *Late 19th century*

I know nothing except the fact of my ignorance. *Socrates (c. 470–399 BCE)*

34. Familiarity breeds contempt

Late 14th century

The idea that familiarity breeds contempt is an odd example of a saying that is more widely repeated than believed. Studies have shown that people actually tend to think that the more they know about people, the more probable it is that they will like them. However, recent work led by Michael I. Norton at Harvard Business School suggests that in this respect we are hopeless optimists: actually, the more we know about people, the more likely we are to take against them.[4]

Norton's explanation for this centres on the ambiguity effect. When we don't know a lot about other people, it is easy for us to fill in the gaps which make them seem more agreeable to us. In practice, this usually means thinking they are similar to us. We imagine they share our tastes, sense of humour and world view, but only because they seem superficially nice and we have no evidence that they don't share them. However, the more information we uncover about them, the more likely it is that we will stumble across something that we actively dislike. Hence people tended to rate strangers higher when given a short list of personality descriptors than a long one. It also explains why, when people meet through dating websites, the reality is almost always disappointing.

But the research clarifies more than it simply vindicates

the old adage. Familiarity does not breed contempt by an iron law of diminishing returns. It is not familiarity *per se* which is the problem, but the increased probability of discovering dislikeable characteristics. If these negatives aren't significant, or if there are many unknown positives, there is nothing about getting to know something or someone better which is going to cause you to dislike them.

We needn't therefore fear over-exposure to people or things which we truly do love. As long as we do not have an idealized view of them and expect to find no flaws, there is nothing inevitable about contempt following familiarity. If it did, Mark Twain would not be able to quip that 'Familiarity breeds contempt – and children.'

Compare and contrast

Absence makes the heart grow fonder. *Mid 19th century*

Absence leads to forgetting. *Spanish proverb*

From far away and beloved is better than close by and arguing. *Greek proverb*

35. A foolish consistency is the hobgoblin of little minds

Ralph Waldo Emerson (1803–82)

Years of writing and talking about philosophy have convinced me that rational consistency is not prized highly among the general population. Yet many despise hypocrisy, which is itself a form of inconsistency. This might strike you as inconsistent in itself, but since consistency isn't widely valued, you might not care.

Consistency is simply a matter of avoiding maintaining one thing while simultaneously maintaining or doing something that contradicts it. For example, you're guilty of inconsistency if you say you're not sexist on some occasions but talk or act in a sexist way on others.

Put like that, it might seem obvious that consistency is a good thing. So why the suspicion of it?

One reason is that people misunderstand what it means. It is not inconsistent, for example, to feel like sushi one day and a burger the next. Consistency is not the same as always doing the same thing, regardless of the context. Nor does being consistent mean refusing ever to change your mind. People seem to associate being consistent with being inflexible or dogmatic, whereas in fact, it is the realization that one is being inconsistent that is often a spur to change what one thinks or does.

Hostility to consistency, however, is sometimes rooted in a reasonable concern. Emerson did not speak out against consistency as such, but only that kind of 'foolish consistency' which he called the 'hobgoblin of little minds'. We cannot always be consistent because things are often ambiguous or unknown. To insist on more clarity in thought than there is in the world is foolish, not commendably rational. In such situations, inconsistent beliefs may be truer to the known facts than perfectly consistent ones.

Even when consistency is a virtue, there are surely worse vices than inconsistency in purely theoretical matters. As Jean-Jacques Rousseau put it, 'I would rather be a man of paradoxes than a man of prejudices.'

Compare and contrast

There are no birds in last year's nest. *Early 17th century*

It is the mark of the trained mind never to expect more certainty than the subject matter allows. *Aristotle (384–22 BCE)*

Do I contradict myself? Very well then I contradict myself. (I am large, I contain multitudes.) *Walt Whitman (1819–92)*

36. Life is not a dress rehearsal

Rose Tremain (1943–)[5]

It's easy saying what things are not. Life is not a bed of roses, God is not an old man sitting in a cloud, winning isn't everything. Some negations, however, are more informative than others. Thinking about why an egg is not an elephant won't get you very far, whereas realizing life is not a dress rehearsal might. It's a reminder that this life is a one-shot deal, and if you mess it up, there's no second try.

However, you need to push the metaphor a little further if you are to work out what you've got to do about this. For if life is not a dress rehearsal, is it the main performance or merely an audition? There is an urgency in both, but it is not of the same kind.

The problem with the audition metaphor is that no one really knows the criteria for the casting, or even the nature of the show. Actually, it looks as if there is no director at all, and that the more we attempt to shine in the spotlight, the less able we are to see that the dark stalls are empty.

The idea of audition implies the need to impress someone. But if life is just the show, as long as we're not so bad as to get booed off, why worry about how others judge us? When the curtain comes down, we won't be around to see if we get a standing ovation. But what then is the point of a spectacle without spectators?

The reality is that life is not a dress rehearsal because it is no kind of performance at all. We must act, not in the theatrical sense, but as agents in the real world. The metaphor doubly misleads, because living well takes practice. In that sense, life is a continuous series of dress rehearsals, of trying different things, attempting to improve, all for its own sake, and never with any final, definitive performance.

Compare and contrast

Be happy while y'er leevin, for y'er a long time deid. *Scottish proverb*

Tempus edax rerum (Time the devourer of everything). *Ovid (43 BCE–c. AD 17)*

Gather ye rosebuds while ye may. *Robert Herrick (1591–1674)*

37. Pride comes before a fall

Late 14th century

Of the seven deadly sins, pride is the only one that can today be used positively without any qualification. Gluttony, sloth and envy remain undisputed vices, while wrath is acceptable only at moments of extreme provocation. Lust is widely celebrated, but retains a hint of the forbidden about it, while sentiments like 'Greed is good' still have a whiff of the paradoxical.

Pride, however, is widely declared a good thing. Parents are proud of their children, James Brown sang 'I'm black and I'm proud,' and United Airlines even 'proudly serves Starbucks coffee'. Indeed, when Michelle Obama said that during her husband's election campaign she felt proud to be American for the first time, she was criticized for her tardiness.

Perhaps that is because the biblical sin of pride is somewhat different from the pride we now take in making good coffee. 'Pride goeth before destruction, and a haughty spirit before a fall,' is the phrase in Proverbs 16 which gave birth to our modern saying. Such pride is the kind which puts humanity above its God, and the proud thus fall because God trips them up: 'Every one that is proud in heart is an abomination to the Lord: though hand join in hand, he shall not be unpunished.'

We can still have ideas above our station even if we don't believe in God or any other natural hierarchy. Whenever we believe we have more power and entitlement than we do, we take on the wrong kind of pride. Hubris is a practical as well as a moral failing, because it blinds us to our own weak spots. In contrast, taking pride in what we do can be the perfectly benign desire to do the best we can.

The two prides are not unrelated, however. Pride in country and offspring can be of either variety. If we see our children's achievements as extensions of our own, or believe that we are personally superior to others because of our nationality, the pride we feel exceeds the merit we really have. Whether or not it leads us to trip up, it is bad enough that such pride comes before a fool.

Compare and contrast

The haughty will be laid low; those who lower themselves will be raised up. *Italian proverb*

The arrogant army will lose the battle for sure. *Chinese proverb*

Modesty is the highest form of arrogance. *German proverb*

38. The man who gives little with a smile gives more than the man who gives much with a frown

Jewish proverb

Who is the greater philanthropist? Warren Buffett, who has given away over $30 billion to charity? Bill Gates, who has donated in excess of $28 billion? Or Mrs Olive Jones from Pontypridd, who popped her last 50p into a charity box last weekend?

It depends on how you're judging, and why. If you're trying to decide who deserves more credit, you might be inclined to agree with Jesus, who said of Mrs Jones's first-century Middle Eastern equivalent that she 'hath cast in more than they all: For all these have of their abundance cast in unto the offerings of God: but she of her penury hath cast in all the living that she had.'

If, on the other hand, you're looking at it from the point of view of the sick, the poor and the hungry, to say that it would have been better for them to have received a few pence from their fellow paupers instead of billions from Buffett and Gates is to get charity back to front: it makes it all about the virtue of the benefactor and not the welfare of the beneficiary.

It is true that when you give money directly to someone in need, how you relate to them is very important. It may indeed be worse for a beggar to be tossed pounds dismissively than it is to be handed pence with kindness. When you are an outcast in society, to be treated with respect as a human being counts for a lot. Dignity may not be priceless, but it is not to be sold cheap.

But this ethos does not translate to the world of anonymous giving. To think that your motivations or attitude are of prime importance is to adopt an oddly narcissistic view of charity. People are dying and living miserable lives because relatively rich people won't part with enough of their cash. They need our help and don't care whether you give with a smile or a frown, to impress your peers or out of pure compassion. They just need us to give.

Compare and contrast

He gives twice who gives quickly. *Mid 16th century*

Give me bread and call me stupid. *Spanish saying*

God loveth a cheerful giver. *St Paul, II Corinthians 9:7*

39. It's no use crying over spilt milk

Mid 17th century

If it's no use crying over spilt milk, and downright bizarre to cry when it's unspilt, does that simply mean crying is never any use at all? Only if you think the metaphor could just as easily have been any other misfortune. But perhaps there are good reasons why we talk of spilt milk rather than dropped scones or lost coins.

A cat may pounce on a puddle of cow juice, but for us humans, once it hits the floor, it's ruined. Drop a scone, on the other hand, and you can always pick it up, brush it off and eat it. Go work in a restaurant for a week if you don't believe me.

What's more, dropping some semi-skimmed is hardly a catastrophe. The scale of the misfortune is at least as significant as its irreversibility when deciding how many of your tears it merits.

When a tragedy is greater, crying is not just understandable, but properly human. No one comforts a widow at a graveside by comparing her dead husband to spilt milk. On the other hand, when a misfortune is correctable, tears are not appropriate because with action they are not necessary.

Spilt milk is hence one of the most precise metaphors found in any proverb. This shows that figurative language can be more accurate than the literal. 'What's done cannot be undone' sounds more straightforward, but it is sweepingly wrong, as anyone who has had to backtrack while assembling flat-pack furniture will know.

Even when true, the question still remains, 'So what?' When we cannot undo the past, we still have to deal with it. We may not be able to undo the harm, but we can sometimes make amends. Remorse and sadness are often appropriate reactions, even if they change nothing but ourselves. We don't have to dwell in the past to acknowledge it exists, and still matters in the present. The thought that every past hurt matters as little as spilt milk leaves a sour taste.

Compare and contrast

The past is at least secure. *American proverb, early 19th century*

What is the use of crying when the birds ate the whole farm? *Indian proverb*

Even a god cannot change the past. *Agathon (c. 448–400 BCE)*

40. The unexamined life is not worth living

Plato (c.427–347 BCE)

The idea of nobility suggests elevation of the few over the ignoble many. That is perhaps why if you scratch many a noble ideal you can sniff the unmistakeable aroma of elitism.

The ideal of the examined life is noble for precisely this reason. It sounds unobjectionable: an encouragement to be fully human, to use our highly developed faculty of thought to raise our manner of existence above that of mere beasts. For if we don't think, we are no more than animals, simply eating, sleeping, working and procreating. And though it may be a bit strong to say such lives are not worth living at all, all but a minority agree that they are much less valuable than fully human ones.

However, there would be no need to exhort us to examine life if we did not think that there were human beings who do not undertake this self-examination, and so have valueless, bestial lives. The noble ideal has a harsh implication: some in the herd of humankind may as well be animals, or dead.

This thought becomes even more chilling when you think about what someone like Plato would consider an examined life to be like. For though almost everyone questions the way they live at some point, it is probably only a minority who subject their lives to Socratic scrutiny. The bulk of humankind, today and in history, has been far too busy struggling for survival to engage in lengthy philosophical analyses of meaning. So if an examined life is more than one in which just a little investigation takes place, by implication, huge swathes of humanity are worthless, ignorant beasts.

Look at many of those who actually appeal to Plato's maxim and you'll find it is quite clear that their message implies that only elites have worthwhile lives, while the great unwashed merely exist. However valuable the examination of life is, to make it a necessary condition of worthwhile existence is to deny the value of millions of your fellow humans' lives.

Compare and contrast

Know thyself. *Inscription on the 6th century* BCE *Temple of Apollo at Delphi*

I do not know myself, and God forbid that I should. *Johann Wolfgang von Goethe (1749–1832)*

To live at all is miracle enough. *Mervyn Peake (1911–68)*

41. Diligence is the mother of good luck

16th century

The saying that Lady Luck is fickle is a horrible mix of the sexist, the anthropomorphic and the tautologous. The anthropomorphism is misleading, because the whole point about luck is that is random, unthinking and has no intentions to be fickle about. And if that's all we mean, then we are left with an empty tautology: there is nothing to luck but luck.

Yet at the same time we often hear that you make your own luck, particularly in sport. For instance, fortune did indeed seem to favour the brave when Manchester United battled to the last to rob Bayern Munich of the Champions League trophy in 1999. But when West Bromwich Albion just escaped relegation from the Premier League in 2005, thanks largely to favourable results at three other games on the last day of the season, their managers' claim that they had made their own luck seemed less credible.

So is luck beyond or within our power to control? Some things we can alter and some we can't, and knowing which is which is crucial to navigating through life's obstacles. That's why even non-believers can see the truth in the opening words of Reinhold Niebuhr's serenity prayer: 'God grant me the serenity to accept the things I cannot change; courage to change the things I can; and wisdom to know the difference.'

Recognizing the limits of our ability to make our own luck is central to understanding this difference. Some things are not down to luck at all, but our own deeds. In other cases such as that of West Brom, the role of diligence is not to eliminate the random, but to make sure that you are ready to grasp the benefits if luck comes your way. In both cases, diligence pays.

However, no amount of diligence can change the outcome of events beyond our control. If two sporting teams, for example, both work as hard as each other to make sure they are able to capitalize on any good fortune that befalls them, luck will determine their fates, not endeavour. Hard work can mitigate the effects of luck, but it cannot eliminate them altogether.

Compare and contrast

The devil's children have the devil's luck. *Early 18th century*

The bone doesn't come to the dog, but the dog goes to the bone. *German proverb*

There is no bad weather only bad clothing. *Swedish proverb*

42. A little learning is a dangerous thing

Alexander Pope (1688–1744)

Witty and apposite replies are always most effective when immediate. But sometimes it is worth waiting 150 years for the right one. So it is that in the nineteenth century the great scientist T. H. Huxley finally asked, 'If a little knowledge is dangerous, where is the man who has so much as to be out of danger?'

The question cuts to the quick of the problem with Pope. His original insight was that to have a partial understanding of something can be misleading. What you still don't know could be more important than what you do, but you might be led into a false sense of certainty by the fact that you do at least know something. So it was that Rumsfeld's known knowns led him to jump to conclusions about the known unknowns and to misunderestimate the importance of the unknown unknowns. And there is no shortage of people whose little knowledge of the untruths Blair said in the build-up to war gives them great confidence that he is a liar.

On this, Huxley and Pope would have been in agreement. Huxley's concern was that, nonetheless, given that the danger of a little learning derives from its incompleteness, and no one has complete knowledge, how can we ever be safe?

The answer is, of course, that we can't. But that is no

cause for despair. Often, we can see enough of the whole picture to make out what it is, even if all the pieces of the jigsaw are not in place. The more complete it is, the greater confidence we can have, even if we can never be totally sure what slotting in the last piece will reveal.

Less obviously, but more importantly, Pope's warning is not about ignorance in itself, but lack of awareness of our ignorance. We must always be mindful of what we don't yet know, whether we are already cognizant of a little or a great deal. A lot of knowledge can also be a dangerous thing, if we mistake it for the whole truth.

Compare and contrast

In the country of the blind the one-eyed man is king. *Early 16th century*

Knowledge takes up no space. *Spanish proverb*

He who knows does not speak. He who speaks does not know. *Lao Tzu (c.604–531 BCE)*

43. Ask not what your country can do for you – ask what you can do for your country

John F. Kennedy (1917–1963)

Whether JFK's secular sainthood is deserved, there is no doubt that his inaugural speech of 1960 was a classic appeal to the better selves of his fellow countrymen. One line provided a formula that has been recycled and revised countless times since: Ask not what your country/school/company/family/church/etc. can do for you – ask what you can do for it.

The sentence's power to evoke a sense of higher purpose is so strong it is easily hijacked to defend power and privilege, rather than the common good. Calls to serve one's country can easily be a ploy to get people to serve the interests of the state, monarch, or other leaders.

However, it would be another kind of error to think that the common good we are being called on to serve is a collective. The phrase would not have struck a chord in America's ruggedly individualistic culture if that was its intended meaning.

What then is the true spirit of JFK's appeal? The context was the realization that 'man holds in his mortal hands the power to abolish all forms of human poverty' as well as 'all forms of human life'. In the Cold War, there seemed two possible futures: the triumph of freedom and prosperity or the annihilation of both, if not the entire human race.

Kennedy's call to his fellow Americans was therefore followed by one to 'My fellow citizens of the world: ask not what America will do for you, but what together we can do for the freedom of man.' JFK was appealing to people to rally around a common purpose, not because collectives are more valuable than individuals, but because in order for individuals to preserve their freedoms, collective action was necessary. For Americans, 'your country' is never an amorphous mass, but a collection of free individuals. That is why whenever JFK's words are bastardized so as to suggest that we should put the group before its members, his legacy is not honoured, but undermined.

Compare and contrast

Dulce et decorum est pro patria mori (It is sweet and fitting to die for one's country). *Horace (65–8 BCE)*

Never was a patriot yet, but was a fool. *John Dryden (1631–1700)*

Patriotism is the last refuge of a scoundrel. *Samuel Johnson (1709–84)*

44. Love is blind

Late 14th century

What is love?

Love can be Cupid, often portrayed as blind, and hence the origins of this saying. The idea is that whoever the God of Love hits with his arrows is decided more or less randomly. Certainly infatuation often does ignore such trivialities as whether the person is really nice or suitable. However, that old killjoy science has studied attraction for some years now and shown that it is the opposite of blind when it comes to superficial indicators of fitness, such as wealth and beauty. There is enough variation in human beings for plenty of surprise combinations still to emerge, but most of the time we are all too predictable.

If love is the intense emotion felt especially at the start of a relationship, then science this time supports the old adage. In romantic love, the area of the brain most concerned with arousal, the hypothalamus, is more active, while areas which control critical thinking and judgement, located mainly in the right hemisphere, are deactivated.[6] (Interestingly, maternal love also involves this suppression of critical thought, hence the Neapolitan saying, 'even a cockroach is beautiful to its mother'.) However, this kind of intense romantic love is said to last typically for only two years, after which time our critical faculties come back and love can see all too clearly again.

Whether this is unfortunate or not depends on which side of the veil you are standing.

But what if love is the enduring bond between two people which keeps them together after the first flush of passion has passed? This is often called companionate love, but that name fails to capture the true affection, warmth and indeed passion that it often involves. This kind of love is thankfully not blind. The truest love sees the lover for who he or she is and loves him or her all the more for it. What infatuation doesn't see, love simply chooses to tolerate and accept.

Compare and contrast

One cannot love and be wise. *Early 16th century*

Marry in haste and repent at leisure. *Mid 16th century*

The good marriage lasts three days – and the bad lasts until death. *Italian proverb*

45. Neither a borrower
nor a lender be

William Shakespeare (1564–1616)

Some timeless advice is more honoured in the breach than the observance, usually because it is easier said than done. For who would borrow if they didn't have to? And without the needs of borrowers, what would be the profit in lending?

As is the case in many sayings in this book, provenance as well as practicality also cautions against taking this particular maxim too earnestly. In *Hamlet*, Shakespeare's independent financial adviser is Polonius, a foolish old windbag whom people laugh at and never with. His counsel is part of a cautionary farewell to his son, where prudence and the maintenance of good reputation seem to be the only underlying principles. The final injunction, 'to thine own self be true' is an ironic triumph of preaching over practice. What's more, Polonius is a nobleman, and those of humbler birth may find emulating his pecuniary austerity more difficult.

Economists warn that following Polonius's advice on a grand scale would lead to a much less efficient and productive economy. The 2008 global credit crunch may well have made us doubt this, but the core problem was surely one of excess and imbalance, not of lending *per se*. Starvation is not the long-term remedy for obesity, and banning loans is not the right way to stop bad ones.

There is also an ethical argument for at least some lending. A world in which no one borrows is one in which people are more self-contained and less dependent on others. There are advantages to this, of course, but in an age where the atomization of society is an increasing problem, it is odd to advocate even less interconnectedness.

On a practical level, lending on a small scale is probably one of the most effective ways of helping the poor to help themselves. Micro-credit schemes, such as those pioneered by Nobel Peace Prize-winner Muhammad Yunus, use loans which enable rather than disable borrowers.

Borrowing and lending are only a problem when exploitative or unaffordable. Otherwise, this can be a practical and dignified way of making the best use of resources, one which allows those with less to move forward without the need for charity.

Compare and contrast

He that goes a-borrowing, goes a-sorrowing. *Late 15th century*

Lend your money and lose your friend. *Late 15th century*

Good accounts make good friends. *French proverb*

46. Beauty is in the eye of the beholder

Mid 18th century

It is the mark of the dull mind to mistake a conversation opener for its last word. Saying that beauty is in the eye of the beholder is so often taken to be the pearl of wisdom that ends debate, leaving us with the need to accept that tastes vary and that is all that can be said. But although accepting the subjectivity of aesthetic judgement may close off some fields of objective enquiry, it opens up another which is at least as fertile.

Take human beauty. It may well be in the eye of the beholder, but it is also nonetheless true that our eyes tend to agree on a great deal. If I were to ask a hundred people to rank pictures of ten very different-looking people according to their beauty, I bet you could make an accurate guess as to which, on average, were ranked the highest. What is more, we can actually identify the kind of objective characteristics that mean that someone like George Clooney will almost always be considered more attractive than I will. In other words, our subjective impressions of beauty are at least in part the product of objective facts about human nature, the social world and how things actually look. So in some sense, beauty really is 'out there' as well as in the mind's eye.

It is also the case that the significance of beauty varies

according to what it is we're talking about. When we debate art or music, for example, we are often concerned with more than just whether it strikes us as beautiful. Arts criticism is only partly about taste and personal judgement. It is also about form, structure, meaning, historical and social context, technique and so on.

What the dull mind misses is that the eye of the beholder is itself a fascinating subject for objective investigation; and there is much more outside of it to explore once beauty has been taken care of.

Compare and contrast

De gustibus et coloribus non est disputandum (Tastes and colours cannot be questioned). *Latin proverb*

'A matter of taste' says the monkey and bites into soap. *German saying*

Some like the priest, some like the wife of the priest. *Hungarian saying*

47. Happiness depends upon ourselves

Aristotle (384–322 BCE)

Take a look around the self-help section of your local book-shop and you might think Aristotle was right. Everything you need to be happy is apparently within your reach. Take charge of your life and you can win friends, lose weight, gain confidence, achieve your goals and have great sex.

Except that is not what Aristotle meant at all. Like the stoics of ancient Greece, he thought that happiness required the ability to deal with fickle fortune, not the power to tame it. How we react to events, rather than what those events are, determines whether we are truly happy.

The self-help culture of the present day, in contrast, promises us that we can seize control, not of our responses to circumstances, but of the circumstances themselves. The idea is not to live with failures and disappointments but to avoid them altogether. We should not rise above the tides of fortune but try to control them. Canute, however, is a poor guide to wise living.

Aristotle was not an advocate of a passive fatalism. On the contrary, he thought that the good person should strive to live a good life and that those who did so would be happier than those who did not. But although we can shape events, the only thing we are entirely in control of is how we react to them, which is why we need to get that right above all if we are to be sovereigns of our own contentment.

The message is a valuable counterweight to the hollow promises of glossy magazines and advertisers. But it can be taken too literally. Sometimes, happiness is not within our control. Although antidepressant drugs may well be over pre-scribed, there are at least some cases when people are miserable due to nothing more than a chemical imbalance in their brains. To such a person, Aristotle's wisdom could be as useless as the latest self-help bestseller.

Compare and contrast

Every man is the architect of his own fortune. *Mid 16th century*

Let tears flow of their own accord: their flowing is not incon-sistent with inward peace and harmony. *Seneca (4 BCE–AD 65)*

Nothing happens to any man that he is not formed by nature to bear. *Marcus Aurelius (121–80)*

48. If it ain't broke, don't fix it

Late 20th century

Doing nothing is a much underrated inactivity. When the cry of 'something must be done' goes out, it is always worth stopping to ask why. As Joseph Conrad said, action 'is the enemy of thought and the friend of flattering illusions'. It can make us feel we are dealing with a problem even if in reality we are making it worse, or even avoiding it. For example, I was recently told of passengers at a temporarily closed train station being advised to take a long diversion rather than wait at the station for services to resume, almost certainly extending their total journey time. But as a staff member explained, they suggested it because 'People like to move.'

The bias towards action over inaction is most evident in the political sphere. It is a rare and brave politician who says, 'This issue is extremely important. But since the only measures on the table right now would probably just make matters worse, or at most no better, the best thing to do is nothing at all.' The leader who says something must and can be done looks decisive and strong; the one who says nothing can or should be done looks weak and unimaginative.

There is, however, the danger of making the opposite mistake and overrating the merits of inactivity. After all, a stitch in time saves nine. It is often worth 'fixing' something that isn't yet broken in order to avoid terminal failure sometime in the future.

More fundamentally, the idea that the unbroken should be left alone can actually be anti-progressive conservatism masquerading as common sense. The fact that feudalism, slavery and unelected absolute monarchies all functioned would have been a bad argument for their retention. If they work against the interests of oppressed minorities or even majorities, or if alternatives would work even better, then fixing them would be precisely the right thing to do. Just because something isn't broken, it doesn't mean we should want it as it is.

Compare and contrast

When in doubt, do nowt. *Mid 19th century*

He who leaves the manor loses his seat. *Spanish proverb*

Everything new, everything beautiful. *French saying*

49. Youth is wasted on the young

George Bernard Shaw (1856–1950)

People are so good at wasting whatever it is they happen to have in abundance that it seems unfair to single out the young for their profligacy. Couldn't we equally say that money is wasted on the rich, luck squandered on the lucky, or beauty frittered away on the beautiful? There are innumerable pairs of a noun and its corresponding adjective that can be inserted into the form of this saying, each generating a statement that rings true.

'Youth' and 'young' however, arguably produce one of the more dubious propositions. The complaint of older people is that the young have vitality, health, no responsibilities, and a whole world of possibilities before them, yet they fail to take full advantage of these blessings.

However, given the nature of youth, this is inevitable. For instance, to have no responsibilities is to be free to live without care for the long term or even what tomorrow might bring. But whereas youth's lack of responsibility is an absence of something yet to come, the independence we crave when old requires the removal of something that has long hampered us. Those who find themselves unburdened of responsibilities they have shouldered for years will of course be more alive to the full potential of this liberty. Freedom feels more real to those who were once in chains. The young cannot then be expected to fully appreciate the value of liberty. Only those who have been deprived of the carefreeness of youth, or the few who are precociously wise, learn to appreciate it properly before they grow old.

'Youth is wasted on the young' has to be understood as paradoxical and ironic. If we truly think that youth is a blessing, then we must see the wasting of it by the young as an inevitable sign that their youth remains uncorrupted by bitter experience, and so smile on their prodigality, not weep over it.

Compare and contrast

If youth but knew, if old age but could. *French proverb*

Some wish they had a beard and the ones that do, are spitting on it. *Greek proverb*

The owl of Minerva spreads its wings only with the falling of the dusk. *G. W. F. Hegel (1770–1831)*

50. You can't judge a book by its cover

Early 20th century

We know that appearances can be deceptive. All that glitters is not gold, for example. However, there comes a point where we see enough of the appearance to conclude that it is indeed the reality: 'If it looks like a duck, walks like a duck and quacks like a duck, then it may just be a duck.'

The attributed author of this quote is actually a good test case of its value and limitations. Walter Reuther was supposed to have said it during the McCarthy era, as an explanation of how you spot a communist. But Reuther was not a stereotypical McCarthyite. He was a Democrat, a trade unionist who fought all his life for workers' rights, and an early environmental campaigner, instrumental in the cleaning up of Lake Erie.

Reuther is thus a good example of how appearances deceive, but only if you don't pay enough attention to them. Simply notice his fierce anti-communism and you'd get him wrong. But look at the totality of what he did, and you'll get the man pretty right. The duck test works, but only if you examine how it looks, moves and sounds. Any one indicator by itself could be misleading. Similarly, it may be rash to judge a book by its cover, but there is no esoteric essence which remains unknown after you've read its contents as well. It is as it appears.

The fact that appearances *can* be deceptive does not mean there is always more to anything than can ever meet the eye. What are you left with when you strip away how something acts, talks, looks, tastes, feels and smells? Only what the Irish philosopher George Berkeley disparagingly called 'something, I know not what'.

It is perhaps too strong to say that everything is nothing more than the sum total of its appearances. But we can only judge anything or anyone on what it is possible to observe, and if we look long and hard enough, such judgements are as reliable as any.

Compare and contrast

The habit does not make the monk. *Italian proverb*

It's not only cooks who have long knives. *Dutch proverb*

At fifty, everyone has the face he deserves. *George Orwell (1903–50)*

51. All men are rapists

Marilyn French (1929)

We don't just take for granted sayings and quotations we assume to be true. Certain notorious utterances take on the opposite quality: they become examples of self-evident nonsense, to be held up as proof of how idiotic people can be. Marilyn French's famous comment that all men are rapists is one such phrase which has been ridiculed as evidence of the daftness of militant feminism.

However, when an obviously ridiculous view is attributed to any group, be suspicious. In this case, the first thing you need to know is that French's line is spoken by a character in her novel *The Women's Room*. It is an extreme expression of a more moderate view, that sees male sexuality as potentially dark and oppressive.

Andrea Dworkin gave one example of this when she wrote, 'Seduction is often difficult to distinguish from rape. In seduction, the rapist bothers to buy a bottle of wine.' There is an uncomfortable truth lurking here, if one dares to look for it.

Consider first of all the use of date rape drugs like GHB and Rohypnol. To slip one of these into someone's drink and then have sex with them while they are virtually unconscious is obviously rape, and no sane person would defend it. But now consider the tactic of trying to get the person you aim to seduce drunk. This is very common, and people often joke about it.

The key difference between drug-rape and booze-rape is obviously that the person consuming the alcohol chooses to do so. But how wide is the gap between the sober 'seducer' who continues to ply an already drunk target and the date-rapist who spikes the drink?

There are serious issues at stake here. However, the effect of constantly trotting out the 'all men are rapists' line is that feminist concerns about male sexuality can be held up as extreme and absurd. It's one of the oldest tricks in the rhetorical book: put words into someone's mouth and then condemn her for saying them.

Compare and contrast

There is no such thing as society. *Margaret Thatcher (1925–), widely quoted without the continuation, 'There are individual men and women, and there are families'*

There are some fucks for which a person would have their partner and children drown in a frozen sea. *Hanif Kureshi (1954–) – or rather one of his characters in* Intimacy

Ninety-five per cent of women's experiences are about being a victim. Or about being an underdog, or having to survive. *Jodie Foster (1962–), widely quoted without the first clause, 'And in terms of women in history . . .'*

52. Lightning never strikes the same place twice

Mid 19th century

When an expression which almost everyone knows is false persists for so long, asking why is probably more interesting than probing the saying directly.

People have known for centuries that lightning not only sometimes strikes twice in the same place, it usually does. Lightning will always seek the shortest route to earth, so the highest conductive object in any given area will usually be the one hit in a storm. That's why lightning rods are affixed to church spires.

At the symbolic level, however, lightning strikes still stand for the most potent, unpredictable and uncontrollable forces of fate. No wonder that the Gods have often been thought of as their causes: more than natural, they seem supernatural.

Even if strokes of bad luck were as random as these metaphorical strikes of lightning, it would be illogical to use this unpredictability as a reason to predict they will not happen again. Lady Luck is more amnesiac than fickle, and she does not remember who has already had it tough when she dishes out new misfortunes. A lightning strike is not like a disease which, once suffered, leaves you immune.

It's better to think about the predictability rather than unpredictability of electrical storms. We need to look around and check whether we inadvertently made ourselves targets. Once struck, twice shy. People talk about bolts from the blue, but thunderstorms do not just appear above us unannounced. Did we fail to heed the signs? Did we perhaps leave ourselves dangerously exposed, standing where we were most likely to be hit? If we can't help but live somewhere vulnerable, could not the timely installation of a rod have saved us?

These questions are all metaphorical of course. But they are useful metaphors, ones that ask hard questions about the world as it is and our place in it. Random bad luck is all too real, but so is the pain of people being hit by misfortune again and again because they cannot see they have made lightning rods for their own backs.

Compare and contrast

It never rains but it pours. *Early 18th century*

No storm lasts long. *Spanish proverb*

There seldom is a single wave. *Icelandic proverb*

53. He that is without sin among you, let him first cast a stone

John 8:7

Several years ago, British television screened a drama based on a frequently recycled premise: what if Jesus were to come back today? In this one, I recall the messiah was Glaswegian. One scene updated the Gospel story of the crowd who brought a woman to Jesus and said, 'Master, this woman was taken in adultery, in the very act. Now Moses in the law commanded us, that such should be stoned: but what sayest thou?' Jesus thought about it for a long time, just drawing in the sand, before replying, 'He that is without sin among you, let him first cast a stone at her.' The crowd then slowly dispersed, leaving the woman unharmed. 'Go, and sin no more,' Jesus told her.

In the Scottish version, Jesus comes across a group of men about to lay into an adulterous woman they were calling a slag and whore. This time, they don't ask for advice, but Christ simply says, 'Have you nae done it yourselves?'

The updating here is, I think, quite insightful. We have come to think of 'He who is without sin . . .' as a general exhortation never to judge others. But if that were the case, it would be unworkable. Imagine a country where thieves, attackers and murderers never faced justice because the only people qualified to dispense it were the spotlessly innocent.

The gospel origins of the phrase do not support this global quietism. While it would be too literal to say that the advice applies only to stoning and adultery, it would be equally foolish to assume the precise situation was irrelevant. The original case is an apt example for the more general message because it is an example of an extreme punishment for a common indiscretion. In such cases, harsh condemnation is both hypocritical and disproportionate.

The injunction not to cast the first stone should not be read as a plea always to turn a blind eye. It is simply a reminder not to be harsher on others than we would have them be on ourselves, and to make sure that any punishment we do mete out fits the crime. Casting stones may be the prerogative of the blameless, but issuing fines does not require the same purity.

Compare and contrast

The pot calling the kettle black. *Late 17th century*

The owl calls the sparrow big-headed. *Hungarian proverb*

He that first cries out to stop thief, is often he that has stolen the treasure. *William Congreve (1670–1729)*

54. What the eye doesn't see, the heart doesn't grieve over

16th century

If you think what you don't know can't hurt you, talk to a hepatologist. The liver contains no pain receptors, which is why people who drink about a bottle of wine a day for ten years and are thus at high risk of liver disease, can know nothing about the worsening condition of their internal organ until it's too late. Like bullets flying towards the back of the head and stealth taxes, the impact of liver disease is not diminished by our ignorance about it.

The idea that the heart doesn't grieve over what the eye doesn't see, however, is importantly different. The point is that the drinker slowly pickling her liver doesn't lose any sleep over her worsening condition, just as the payer of stealth taxes remains blissfully unaware of her surreptitious impoverishment. In both cases the harm is real, but it causes no distress. Ignorance is bliss but is a fool's paradise.

But what of the things the eye not only doesn't see, but will never see? The infidelity that for ever remains a secret, the back-stabbing bitching that never gets back to its victim, or any number of unshattered illusions we have about ourselves or others? What is the point of bringing these truths to the attention of people they will hurt, if they will be happier not knowing?

Such dilemmas can be resolved only case by case. But the fact that people will be happy not knowing does not clinch it. A deprivation is no less real just because one doesn't know what one is deprived of. Some would rather not know unpleasant truths while others would always choose the truth over ignorant contentment. There may be no merit in telling someone a truth they don't want to hear, but to withhold one they would want to know is in some ways to really harm someone, because it diminishes their capacity to live as they would chose.

Compare and contrast

Out of sight, out of mind. *Mid 13th century*

A slice off a cut loaf isn't missed. *Late 16th century*

Far from the eyes, far from the heart. *French proverb*

55. It's better to burn out than fade away

Neil Young (1945–)

It is not just rock and rollers who have railed against life ending in a damp squib. Dylan Thomas urged, 'Do not go gentle into that good night. Rage, rage against the dying of the light.' Likewise, when T. S. Eliot wrote that the world ends 'not with a bang but a whimper', he wasn't trying to cheer us up.

But is this what we really think? Ask the question, 'Is it better to burn out than fade away?' and many people will say yes. But ask the question, 'How would you like to die?' and most reply, 'Peacefully in my sleep, at a ripe old age,' as the various celebrity Q&As in the weekend supplements will testify.

The truth behind the rhymes of Young and Thomas is that it is better to reach your life's end with all its credit spent. That idea is also reflected in a line from Ridley Scott's *Blade Runner*: 'The light that burns twice as bright burns half as long.' What matters is not the length of the life but that, at the end, all its available light has been used up.

That is far removed from the naively romantic rock and roll desire to live fast and die young. Roger Daltry once hoped he would die before he got old, but now he's drawing his pension, he is quite rightly pleased he didn't get what he once hoped for.

Dying too soon is as much of a waste as living long and frittering your time away. Neil Young knew that, which is why as well as 'My My, Hey Hey', he also wrote a song called 'The Needle and the Damage Done', which is a lament for lives cut short by heroin abuse. It's not the length or speed of life, nor the manner of one's death that really counts. It's that, when the final reckoning comes, there's no wick on life's candle left to burn.

Compare and contrast

God calls whom he loves. *Spanish proverb*

Everything has an end, only a sausage has two. *German proverb*

Death will find me alive. *Italian proverb*

56. Worry is interest paid on trouble before it is due

Early 20th century

Worry is the Facebook of the emotions – few can see the point of it, but many get caught up in it. 'What's the use of worrying?' British soldiers sang as they lined up to get slaughtered in the trenches of the First World War. 'It never was worthwhile.' No amount of troubled concern could have saved those who were killed. All it would have done was made their last days on earth even more hellish than they already were.

But now imagine the generals plotting their campaign. Perhaps one of them, considering the implications of one plan, says that he is concerned that his men will be turned into cannon fodder if the attack goes ahead. To give him a slap on the back and say that worrying never was worthwhile would not be wise counsel, but grotesque disrespect for life.

The difference between the generals and the Tommys is that only the worry of those in a position to change things can save the soldiers' lives. Worry is fruitless only when it cannot help effect a change. But when it can lead to revisions which make things better, worry is invaluable.

That's why governments have professional worriers to think about all manner of frightening contingencies, so as to make sure the country is prepared for the worst. Worrying allows us to anticipate trouble, and so deal with it more effectively. For instance, if the right people had been worrying about the right things, then perhaps the 2008 credit crunch would have had less of a bite.

The snag is that there is no clean distinction between the potential disasters we cannot avert and those we can. Moreover, we have to take account of probabilities, otherwise we'd spend all our lives protecting ourselves against catastrophes that are very unlikely to befall us. Yet we are not on the whole very good at either accepting there are things we cannot change, or making rational decisions on a probabilistic basis. That's why we often worry more than we should. But the suggestion that we should not worry at all is one we should find very worrying indeed.

Compare and contrast

Don't cross the bridge till you come to it. *Mid 19th century*

He that follows freits [omens], freits will follow him. *Scottish proverb, early 18th century*

Don't worry about eggs that haven't been laid. *German proverb*

57. If God does not exist, everything is permitted

Fyodor Dostoyevsky (1821–81)

In *The Brothers Karamazov*, Ivan speaks for many when he claims that there are no moral limits on what we could do in a Godless universe. For the countless non-believers who deny that ethical atheism is an oxymoron, however, Ivan's claim is a manifest falsehood, a terrible slur on the irreligious. When the same statement is seen as both obviously true and false, that's usually a sign that there is nothing obvious about the matter at all.

What is demonstrably false is the idea that, for all atheists, anything goes. G. K. Chesterton claimed this unambiguously when he reportedly said, 'When men stop believing in God they don't believe in nothing; they believe in anything.' Often, quite the opposite is true. Many are led to give up belief in God, rightly or wrongly, because they feel compelled to do so by the weight of evidence and argument. Anyone with such a commitment to believe only what there are good reasons to believe is clearly not going to believe in just anything.

The assumption that atheists are creedal anarchists when it comes to morality is just as misguided. Even if moral laws are not handed down by a higher authority, secular humanists have many other reasons to be good, and can be as passionate about injustice and wrongdoing as anyone.

But that doesn't mean Ivan is simply wrong. There is one sense in which everything is permitted when God goes. Without God, there is no external authority to impose morality on fallen humankind. As Woody Allen's *Crimes and Misdemeanours* shows, if we do wrong in a godless universe and keep our transgression a secret, we will get away with it.

If we take Ivan's words to mean that, without God, no evil is so great that it will necessarily be punished, we are right. We go wrong only if we think that means it is not possible to have a humanist morality which is our responsibility to uphold.

Compare and contrast

'Twas only fear first in the world made gods. *Ben Jonson (c. 1573–1637)*

If God did not exist, it would be necessary to invent him. *Voltaire (1694–1778)*

God is a thought who makes crooked all that is straight. *Friedrich Nietzsche (1844–1900)*

58. Better the devil you know than the devil you don't know

Mid 19th century

The unknown is always a gamble. Try it, and you could be in for a nasty shock. Pass it by and you may lose a unique opportunity to enrich your life. So what are we to do?

Much quoted is Robert Frost, who claimed to have benefited from having taken the road less travelled. An Italian proverb takes the same metaphor but gives it a different spin: *Chi lascia la via vecchia per la nuova sa quel che lascia ma non sa quel che trova* (He who leaves the old way for the new knows what he is leaving but not what he will find). This is usually offered as a caution, but it could equally be seen as merely descriptive, not prescriptive. That you already know what you're leaving could be a reason for seeking something new, as well as for staying put.

At the most cautious end of the spectrum is the idea that we are better off with the devil we know. Indeed, it is hard to think of a more conservative piece of advice. You would have thought that if you were going to risk the unknown at all, you would do so when the known is terrible. But, no, even when the familiar is satanic, we are told we're better off where we are.

The saying perhaps makes more sense when both devils are taken into consideration. Faced with a choice, it is indeed better to stay with the demon you know something about, so at least you are prepared for his more devious schemes. But what if the choice is between the known devil and the unknown stranger? There is a risk, but in such cases, isn't knowing what you're leaving behind all the more reason to try something new? It is one thing to dance with the devil at Hades ball, quite another to bop with Beelzebub when saints and mortals sit idly by.

Compare and contrast

He who sups with the Devil should have a long spoon. *Late 14th century*

Keep your friends close, and your enemies closer. *Sun Tzu (400–320 BCE)*

Better to live with the Devil than with a mean woman. *Greek proverb*

59. I think, therefore I am

René Descartes (1596–1650)

The most famous line in philosophy sounds clear enough. But what does it really mean? Why, for example, did Descartes write 'I *think*, therefore I am' rather than 'I'm sexually aroused, therefore I am, baby' or 'I punch, therefore I am'?

Descartes focused on thinking because it was his consciousness of what he was doing that justified his firm conclusion that he must exist. 'I punch, therefore I am' works as an argument only if you are *aware* that you are punching. And, of course, your awareness is a kind of thinking. So it is really the fact that you *think* you're punching that shows you must exist, not the fact that you are actually engaged in a brawl.

Nevertheless, having reached this conclusion, what more are you entitled to conclude? Many critics have argued that Descartes got carried away. He maintained that his argument showed that we are *res cogitans* – thinking things – not material bodies – *res extensa*. In short, Madonna may be living in a material world, but she is a mental, not a material, girl.

But surely that assumes too much. All Descartes' argument shows is that he exists at the time he is thinking, and that thinking is one of the things he does. It cannot show that he is therefore not essentially material. Perhaps, for example, he cannot think without his physical brain.

The root of the problem is that nothing can be known about the 'I' in 'I think' other than the fact that it exists at the time of the thinking. Nothing follows from that about its past and future existence at other times, or its fundamental nature now. The 'I' stands alone, certain only of itself at a particular dot in space and time. The certainty of 'I think therefore I am' is thus of an extremely limited kind and it doesn't reveal anything about what kind of creatures we fundamentally are, were, or will be.

Compare and contrast

I never could find any man who could think for two minutes together. *Sydney Smith (1771–1845)*

I think that I think, therefore I think that I am. *Ambrose Bierce (1842–c.1913)*

I exist, that is all, and I find it nauseating. *Jean-Paul Sartre (1905–80)*

60. Follow your heart

Ubiquitous, origin unknown

Three organs battle it out to be the individual's executive decision maker: head, heart and gut. There are those who argue that men have a fourth centre of will which is a little lower, but we'll ignore that for now. The head tells you what reason concludes, the heart what you would like to do, and the gut what your instinct says you should do.

No sensible person believes that in this battle you should always and only trust one organ. Gut is very unreliable, for example, but we rely on it to make split-second decisions that the head doesn't have time to contemplate. In any case, the distinction is somewhat artificial. What we call head, heart and gut are really all functions of the same embodied brain, albeit ones which make use of different regions. To talk of following your heart, as though it were an autonomous centre of desire, is therefore deeply misguided. What we think is affected by how we feel, and vice versa. How much you want to marry your fiancé, for example, will depend on what you know and believe about him.

There is another sense in which the heart sometimes should be led, not followed. When motivation is lacking, it is often inadvisable to just wait until you feel like getting on with whatever it is you want or think you should be doing. Making a reluctant start is often the best way of creating more motivation to carry on. This is even true of the rawest of desires, such as sex. Many couples in long-term relationships lose the spontaneous desire to make love, so they just don't, and as a result, they end up feeling a loss of intimacy which can threaten the relationship. Therapists often advise that the best thing to do is simply get on with it: if you do, you'll find the desire soon returns.

Following your heart is an excellent tie-breaker when your head, informed by gut and heart, is left without a clear decision. But when your heart's not in it, sometimes you need to put it there.

Compare and contrast

Appetite comes from eating. *Spanish proverb*

The heart has its reasons which reason knows nothing of. *Blaise Pascal (1623–62)*

The desires of the heart are as crooked as corkscrews. *W. H. Auden (1907–73)*

61. It is not the man who has too little, but the man who craves more, who is poor

Seneca (3 BCE–AD 65)

It would be comforting to think that there is no one either rich or poor, but thinking makes it so. Consider those living in low-quality, temporary local authority accommodation. Most of us would say they were poor, yet with adequate shelter, clothing, food and healthcare, they are living in luxury compared to many in the developing world or the slums of Victorian Britain. Whether they are poor depends entirely on how you look at it. It's your state of mind, not the state of your finances that counts, a view which much recent psychological research has been used to support.

On a more practical level, it is argued that what really matters is not how limited your means are, but that you live within them. As Dickens's Mr Micawber put it, 'Annual income twenty pounds, annual expenditure nineteen and six, result happiness. Annual income twenty pounds, annual expenditure twenty pounds ought and six, result misery.'

Such an outlook has much to commend it. However, adopted too zealously it can make us forget that there is such a thing as real poverty. The starving person's problem is not that she craves more, it is that she really does not have enough.

Seneca's insight can also be taken as licence to withdraw justifiable concern for those in relative paucity. Why care about people living on the so-called poverty line if they're not *really* poor?

Perhaps most fundamentally, what is wrong with craving more anyway? Desiring further riches for their own sake is certainly futile. But isn't some kind of hunger to squeeze more out of life essential if we are to make the most of our time on earth? The perfectly serene person who is entirely happy with her lot may seem like an ideal to strive towards, but perhaps the price of her peace of mind is that she misses out on what makes life such an incredible adventure in the first place.

Compare and contrast

If you don't have what you love, you have to love what you have. *French proverb*

The more you know, the less you need. *Aboriginal Australian proverb*

Let not your mind run on what you lack as much as on what you have already. *Marcus Aurelius (121–80)*

62. Charity begins at home

Late 14th century

Sometimes sentences stay the same while the words that comprise them change. The meanings of words can shift so slowly and imperceptibly that we can, in saying exactly the same thing for long enough, end up saying something totally different.

Hence in the twenty-first century we have the familiar saying, 'charity begins at home'. You hear it most predictably when people are reluctant to give money to help people in developing countries, victims of foreign wars or natural disasters. What people mean is that you have to look after those closer to you first, and worry about others miles away only second.

It's a defensible principle, but one which has attached itself to the wrong proverb. In the modern sense of the word, 'charity' involves voluntary giving to strangers in need. Giving a bag of rice to an earthquake survivor abroad is charity; cooking rice for your children is not. Charity cannot begin until at least the garden gate, because it has nothing to do with care of kin.

When the phrase first entered circulation, 'charity' still meant something close to the Latin root *caritas*. Often translated as 'Christian love', it is about a kindness to others which has nothing to do with erotic passion or familial duty.

To say that *caritas* begins at home is to say that we cannot hope to be good, kind people if we are not kind to those we share our lives with every day. It may be possible that the Good Samaritan returned home to beat his wife, while the robber who left his victim for dead was a loving family man, but neither is a truly charitable soul.

The key word here is neither charity nor home but *begins*. The whole point of the proverb is that charity does not remain within the confines of our houses. It begins there in order that it may extend far beyond. Far from being a justification for refusing to help strangers overseas, it is really a blueprint for how we might become more naturally inclined to do so more often.

Compare and contrast

The shoemaker's son always goes barefoot. *Mid 16th century*

Keep your own fish-guts for your own sea-maws [gulls]. *Scottish proverb, early 18th century*

For charity is cold in the multitude of possessions, and the rich are covetous of their crumbs. *Christopher Smart (1722–71)*

63. Hell is paved with good intentions

Samuel Johnson (1709–84)[7]

Never let it be said that humankind does not make progress: since Johnson's time, we have managed to extend inferno's paving to cover the road to it as well.

Whichever variant of the saying you choose, good intent gets a pretty bad press. Whenever people pledge to make poverty history, create a more equitable healthcare system, bring peace to the Middle East or take serious steps to protect the environment, dark voices always whisper of the unintended harm such good intentions can cause. When the world stubbornly refuses to get much better overnight, these voices become louder.

While starry-eyed optimism that good results must come from a good heart is undoubtedly dangerous, excessive cynicism about good intentions is hardly any better. After all, we can be sure that heaven is not paved with bad intentions. To want to do the right rather than the wrong thing is at least a start, without which nothing good would ever come at all. Johnson's point was surely not that good intentions always lead to catastrophe, merely that they can do.

Yet his words are often taken as a justification for quietism and despair. Forget about trying to do good or making the world a better place, for your efforts are doomed to make things even worse. The best you can do is let the world go to hell in a handcart and grumble about it in front of the telly. This is not what would be advised by the man who also once said, 'No people can be great who have ceased to be virtuous.' Good intentions by themselves are not enough, but we would do even worse without them.

Compare and contrast

Hell is full of good intentions. *Portuguese proverb*

There is no possibility of thinking of anything at all in the world, or even out of it, which can be regarded as good without qualification, except a good will. *Immanuel Kant (1724–1804)*

All bad art is the result of good intentions. *Oscar Wilde (1854–1900)*

64. To every thing there is a season

Ecclesiastes 3:1

Proverbs send mixed messages about timing. The early bird catches the worm, but he who laughs last laughs longest. He who hesitates is lost, but all things come to those who wait. So what, or rather, when, are we to do?

The Bible tells us it depends. Every thing has its season. The best time of day for worm-catching is early in the morning, and it's better to laugh last than first. Nature has her almanacs and timetables and it is our job to study them.

That certainly removes many of the apparent contradictions found in sayings about timing. The rest can be dissolved by paying closer attention. For example, there is a big difference between hesitating and waiting. The angler, for example, must be prepared to do a lot of the latter, so that when the moment comes, he can dispense with the former and land his catch. Hesitation is the failure to act, waiting is preparation to do so.

Still, there is something unsatisfactory about the advice that everything has its moment. If you ask someone when you should do something, 'at the right time' is hardly informative advice. You may as well advise someone to pick the best dish on the menu, or to try somewhere good for their holiday this year.

There is also a risk of being more constrained by conventional timings than you need be. Is it right to drink port before or after a meal, for example? Are there ages by which a person should have ticked off a list of achievements or life experiences? In the garden, you have to learn to go with the seasons, but in many other areas of life, we are free to fix our own schedule.

Perhaps that is one reason why there are so many different proverbs about timing. Each situation requires us to judge when the right moment is. None of the various sayings can point us to the right answer, but once we have found it, they give us colourful ways of announcing our verdict.

Compare and contrast

The early riser catches the caterpillar. *Spanish proverb*

He who sleeps catches no fish. *Italian proverb*

A windy day is not a day for thatching. *Irish proverb*

65. Can't buy me love'

Paul McCartney (1942–)

The only kind of love that is literally for sale is the euphemistic kind which rock singers can't get enough of, and which Aerosmith sang about enjoying in that most romantic of locations, an elevator. True love, whatever that is, obviously has no price tag.

Does that mean that wealth has no influence at all on whether our love lives flourish or not? It is easy to think that only other people sillier than ourselves allow materialist considerations to influence their choice of life partner. But there is plenty of evidence to suggest that, consciously or not, cash does come into the equation.

The classic example of this is the old, unattractive tycoon and his young, glamorous trophy wife. The men in these partnerships are often criticized for their superficial preference for youth and beauty above maturity and intellect, but the young women themselves are equally shallow if they find power and money so attractive.

This pattern is not easily dismissed as just a quirk of the super-wealthy. For instance, various studies have suggested that economic factors may contribute to divorce. A man who finds himself unemployed for the first time in his life, or whose wife earns a good income, does seem more likely to find himself single again than one who is the undisputed main breadwinner of the partnership. Those men who think that having the right car, watch or clothes will have an effect on how women perceive them are not wholly mistaken.

The troubling thought is that although not many are so transparently materialistic that they consciously think 'He drives an Audi – good husband potential', few of us are so pure in our motives that power, wealth and beauty do not have some bearing on our choice of mate. And if we want to say that anyone influenced by such factors cannot truly be in love, then love is even rarer than we think it is. Money can't buy you love, but sadly it might just help shift the odds in your favour.

Compare and contrast

Pay for love with love; everything else with money. *Spanish proverb*

Love does much, but money does all. *French proverb*

When poverty comes in through the door, love goes out through the window. *Greek proverb*

66. Virtue is its own reward

16th century

Why should we be good? 'Because I say so' is one answer a parent may be tempted to give to her sceptical offspring, backed up with 'because you won't get ice-cream if you're not', if that fails to do the trick.

Theologians may have more subtle answers, but to many it seems God rehearses very similar lines. If 'because I say so' doesn't impress you when it comes from the voice of the deity, then 'because I'll send you to hell if you don't' might make you think twice.

Carrots and sticks are clearly unsatisfactory reasons for doing the right thing. But what other motives could there be? Perhaps we should behave well because to do so is good for us. Enlightened self-interest does not, however, seem to be the same as morality, which is surely defined by the fact that it sometimes requires us to put our own interests second.

It seems hopeless therefore to justify moral imperatives in terms of the rewards they confer on the virtuous, whether they come from authorities, God or direct from good actions themselves. Must then virtue be its own reward?

There is something of the having the cake and eating it about this way out. For it seems to suggest that we should not be virtuous for any benefits that might give us, but that at the same time there is a benefit just in being good. For virtue to be its own reward, there must still be some gain from it.

This seems to be an inescapable fact about morality. However, it does not debunk morality, because we are capable of recognizing that some rewards are so great they matter more even than our own well-being. To give your life for another, for example, makes sense only if you think the prize is worth the loss. So virtue has to have a reward outside of itself after all. It is just that it needn't go to the virtuous.

Compare and contrast

He lives long who lives well. *Mid 16th century*

Whoever leans on a good tree is covered by good shade. *Spanish proverb*

More people are flattered into virtue than bullied out of vice. *R. S. Surtees (1803–64)*

67. Conscience does make cowards of us all

William Shakespeare (1564–1616)

Conscience is under suspicion in the modern West. True, it is still often called upon to justify moral hunches that we don't have the ability or inclination to defend. But often it is also something to be fought, since conscience is the source of guilt, that most negative of emotions.

Guilt is out of fashion because it has been tarnished by dubious associations. In particular, social and religious norms have led many people to feel inappropriately guilty about their sexual acts and desires. Many women are also made to feel guilty either if they don't spend enough time with their children, or if they fail to build successful careers.

But just because guilt is often misplaced, that does not mean that guilt itself is to blame. You might as well decry love, on the grounds that many people love what they should not.

We should likewise be suspicious of the charge against conscience that it turns us into cowards. The popular idea here is that conscience is the brake which stops us doing what we should be bold enough to do. For Hamlet it was avenging his father's murder; for someone today it might be acting on a sexual passion, or seizing an opportunity to advance one's own interests at the expense of a competitor, or colleague.

To call such haltings cowardice, however, is to beg the question. Sometimes we are right to restrain ourselves. Self-control is not the same as pathological repression.

In any case, citing Shakespeare is no help to the anti-conscience cause. What Hamlet called conscience in the famous 'to be, or not to be' soliloquy was not the modern-day moralizing super-ego, but our innermost thoughts more generally. Hence in *Henry V*, Shakespeare puts these words into the mouth of the eponymous hero: 'I will speak my conscience of the king: I think he would not wish himself anywhere but where he is.' This is the conscience of Hamlet. It may well make us cowards, not because it reminds us of our moral duties, but because it also speaks of our irrational, sometimes selfish, fears and neuroses.

Compare and contrast

Faint heart never won fair lady. *Mid 16th century*

Conscience gets a lot of credit that belongs to cold feet. *American proverb, mid 20th century*

Conscience is thoroughly well-bred and soon leaves off talking to those who do not wish to hear it. *Samuel Butler (1835–1902)*

68. Revenge is a dish that can be eaten cold

Late 19th century

Ask someone to complete the saying 'revenge is a dish . . .' and almost everyone will say '. . . best served cold'. Following the culinary metaphor through makes it clear why the difference between this and the original version matters immensely.

Eating gazpacho cold allows you to savour the chilled Spanish soup at its best. Eating a plate of cold leftover pasta, however, mainly avoids waste and the bother of reheating. Few agree that spaghetti bolognese is *best* served cold, even if it *can* be.

This invites the entirely serious question, is revenge more like gazpacho or spaghetti? According to the original saying, the answer is found in Bologna, not Barcelona. Revenge need not be taken immediately and, if necessary, it can wait. Whether or not revenge is something you should take pleasure in is an open question.

The modern variant, however, sees revenge as more like gazpacho, or maybe even as a bowlful of gourmet ice-cream, to be greedily savoured as much as possible.

This is an almost sadistic turn: revenge has gone from being a dirty but sometimes necessary business to something we should schedule to maximize our enjoyment. The move from 'can' to 'best' makes us less likely to see vengeance as undesirable. We may question whether cold pasta is worth serving at all; we are unlikely to ask the same of Ben and Jerry's Chocolate Chip Cookie Dough. Things that are best served cold are generally best served, not thrown out.

The human desire for retribution is very natural, which is why it provides such a compelling narrative for some of our most powerful stage and screen dramas. Yet as these same fictions show, it is a desire that can bring out the worst in us and lead to our downfalls. That's why it is better to think of revenge as something unappetizing that can be dished out cold, rather than something to be salivated over.

Compare and contrast

Don't get mad, get even. *Late 20th Century*

Revenge is always the pleasure of a paltry, feeble, tiny mind. *Juvenal (60–130)*

A man that studieth revenge keeps his own wounds green. *Francis Bacon (1561–1626)*

69. A life spent making mistakes is not only more honourable, but more useful than a life spent doing nothing

George Bernard Shaw (1856–1950)

Shaw's words are reassuring when we survey our own catalogue of mishaps and misadventures. But you don't find too many people who think the Iraq war was a grave mistake talking about Blair and Bush's lives being more honourable and useful as a result of their decision to take us into it. Nor do we hear much praise of error when someone's failings create the opportunity to sue for negligence.

The disparity between our tolerance of our own failings and intolerance of the failings of others is not just a symptom of self-serving bias. It also reflects the genuine but conflicting truths about the role of mistake-making in the good life.

The key is that Shaw is not praising error for its own sake. Making mistakes is superior to doing *no thing*, not the *right thing*. Human beings are fallible, which means if we act, we are going to screw up occasionally. Since a life doing nothing is not worth living, we are forced to conclude that a life of mistakes beats a life of inactivity.

Clearly, however, if two people live equally active lives and the first makes fewer mistakes than the second, it is the first who, all other things being equal, has done better. If making mistakes were better than making right choices, then mistakes would paradoxically become right choices after all.

There is thus a tension between being prepared to accept the inevitability of mistakes as a precondition of action, and the striving to avoid making mistakes wherever possible. When we think of others we tend, unfairly, to accord the avoiding of mistakes the higher priority. But we have an incentive to be more charitable when the mistakes are our own: accepting the inevitability of our errors is probably the most effective way of making them bearable.

Compare and contrast

To err is human. *Late 16th century*

A miss is as good as a mile. *Early 17th century*

If all else fails, immortality can always be assured by a spectacular error. *J. K. Galbraith (1908–2006)*

70. Man is the measure
of all things

Protagoras (c.490–c.420 BCE)

In a competition between an atheist humanist and a religious believer to find the largest ego, it is not immediately obvious whom you should back to win. For all her talk about humility and sense of awe in the face of divine mysteries, the believer still seems to be remarkably confident about her knowledge of the nature of our creator and what he demands of us. To claim to know even part of God's will better than others is hardly modest.

But to the majority, the humanist looks the more arrogant, for she argues that we pathetic little shaven apes have it within our power to understand the world around us, create moral values, and imbue our lives with meaning. To deny any dependence on a higher power when most of us can't even assemble a flat-pack coffee table properly by ourselves appears to be the very definition of hubris.

The phrase 'Man is the measure of all things' looks like the zenith of this arrogance. Are we really so important that everything that exists has to be measured against our scales, our values and our judgement?

But this is not the only way to understand our roles as the cosmic measurers. Rather than assuming any importance for humanity, we should instead start by accepting our helplessness. We are the measure of all things simply because we are unable to access any better yardstick. We do not have access to the mind of the deity nor can we adopt a God's eye view for ourselves. We are condemned to see the world only from a human perspective and no other. We cannot imagine how the world seems to a bat, let alone a deity.

Man is not therefore the measure of all things because of arrogance, but because there is no alternative. Even the religious should agree. For it is overgrown chimpanzees who decide which religion offers the true guide to life, not God.

Compare and contrast

Out of the crooked timber of humanity no straight thing can ever be made. *Immanuel Kant (1724–1804)*

An honest God is the noblest work of man. *Robert G. Ingersoll (1833–1900)*

It is much easier to make measurements than to know exactly what you are measuring. *J. W. N. Sullivan (1886–1937)*

71. You can lead a horse to water, but you can't make him drink

Late 12th century

Dorothy Parker's variant, 'You can lead a horticulture, but you can't make her think,' contains a great deal of truth, even if it unfairly picks on prostitutes. People have realized for many years that learning is most effective when you want to learn. 'Knowledge has to be sucked into the brain, not pushed into it,' as the physicist Victor Weisskopf put it.

That is not, however, quite the same thing as saying that in order to be taught, you must want to be taught. Generations of unwilling schoolchildren will testify that they did indeed learn a great deal in classes they would rather not have attended. The transfer of information in such situations is not maximally efficient, but it does go on.

A failure to appreciate fully the subtle dynamics of push and pull in education arguably led some well-intentioned zealots to leave too much to the pull. Not so long ago, for example, a trainee teacher I know was still being told at a prestigious teacher training college that the best way to deal with students of different abilities was by 'differentiation by outcome'. This means that instead of setting abler students more difficult tasks, you give them the same as the less able, and simply expect them to produce a higher standard response.

You don't need to be an advocate of a return to the 11-plus and caning to realize this is woefully misguided. It is not human nature to expend more effort than is necessary, and brighter children need to be stretched if they are to fulfil their potential. The way to elicit a higher calibre of response is often to ask a more challenging question. The reason for pushing certain things in the brain's direction is to make sure it keeps sucking and doesn't just let out a resigned yawn instead.

In general, there are many things an unwilling horse can be made to do, and for those it can't, nudging, encouraging and cajoling can all make the desired result more likely. Just accepting it won't drink is the mark of the defeatist, not the realist.

Compare and contrast

You can give someone advice, but you can't make him follow it. *Spanish proverb*

At the deaf man's door, knock as much as you like. *Greek proverb*

Go to the square and ask advice; go home and do what you like. *Italian proverb*

72. Nor is the people's judgement always true / The most may err as grossly as the few

John Dryden (1631–1700)

The losers of any election may console themselves that majorities are not always right. Some would go further and agree with Dr Stockmann in Ibsen's *An Enemy of the People*, who declared that 'the majority never has right on its side', because 'the stupid people are in an absolutely overwhelming majority all the world over'.

Even champions of democracy do not usually defend it by appeal to the wisdom of crowds, but by echoing Winston Churchill's view that 'Democracy is the worst form of government except all those other forms that have been tried from time to time.'

Such cynicism rests on the assumption that democracy is premised on the people's capacity to choose wisely. But what if this assumption is false? After all, the most popular songs, books, films or pizzas are far from always the best.

It could be argued that the point of democracy is to give people the kind of government they prefer, not the one that is necessarily best for them. The electorate needs to be able to make mistakes if it is to have true freedom of self-determination. What matters is not that the people choose well, but simply that they choose.

Even if we do desire wise rule, in Western democracies the electorate is not called upon to decide which laws to enact or how to spend the nation's finances. It has the more modest task of picking reasonably smart people capable of making the right choices for it.

But the most important job of the electorate is simply to hold politicians to account. Despite widespread cynicism about politicians, those who flagrantly abuse their power or do nothing for their constituents are usually booted out. The threat of rejection at the ballot box thus gives an incentive to politicians in democracies to work for us and not themselves.

The case for democracy need not rest on the false assumption that the majority is always right, but the credible premise that it helps keep the few who rule in the service of the many.

Compare and contrast

There is safety in numbers. *Late 17th century*

Four eyes see better than two. *German proverb*

Democracy substitutes election by the incompetent many for appointment by the corrupt few. *George Bernard Shaw (1856–1950)*

73. Still waters run deep

Early 15th century

One of my primary school teachers was fond of telling us that 'empty vessels make the most noise'. Since to me a vessel was a boat, I found this puzzling, but understood that she meant us to shut up.

The saying comes from the same century as 'Still waters run deep'. Four hundred years before Freud allegedly 'discovered' the subconscious, the idea that the depths of character could be read from surface personality was already the subject of popular sayings, as was the idea that the outer self could be different from the inner one.

However, only the crudest form of cod psychology would say that these relations between depth and surface hold as universal laws. Still waters may run deep, but the shallowest puddle also makes no waves when undisturbed.

We all know this, but nevertheless, there is a tendency to over-apply the still waters maxim. The illusion of depth appears in many shapes and forms.

For example, when a person presents herself as a blank slate, we are more likely to fill in those blanks for ourselves than assume they are permanently empty. The feeling that there must be more to someone quiet than meets the eye often persists after we have enough evidence to conclude that actually, there probably isn't.

The impression of depth can also be created by tele-graphic or enigmatic utterances that are actually vacuous, but which suggest deeper truths are being unsaid. This kind of intellectual illusion is brilliantly satirized in Hal Ashby's film *Being There*, starring Peter Sellers as a simple-minded gardener called Chance. Chance's brief contributions to conversation are limited to literal, short comments on gardens, such as 'as long as the roots are not severed, all is well', and 'growth has it seasons'. These are taken to be deep, allegorical truths and Chance is mistaken for a wise sage.

The moral can be captured in a statement which is both literally true and allegorical: just because you can't see the bottom, it doesn't mean the well is bottomless.

Compare and contrast

It's the quiet pigs that eat the grain. *Irish proverb*

Hollow barrels sound loudest. *Dutch proverb*

An empty cart rattles louder. *Korean proverb*

74. A man travels the world in search of what he needs and returns home to find it

George Moore (1852–1933)

We may work hard to earn our holidays and look forward to them as the highlight of the year, but many sages have little good to say about travel. For example, back in 1922 G. K. Chesterton turned conventional wisdom on its head when he wrote that 'travel narrows the mind'. The evidence that he is on to something is everywhere, from backpackers roving in mono-national herds, to Brits living in expat ghettos in Spain.

Sections of the cognoscenti have always been wearily dismissive of travel. 'See one promontory (said Socrates of old), one mountain, one sea, one river and see all,' wrote Robert Burton in the 17th century, approvingly. But if the wisest man in Athens really thought Kilimanjaro and Everest were more or less the same, then his famous powers of discernment were not all they were cracked up to be.

Perhaps the most condescending criticism is that the foolish traveller is so busy looking into the distance for what she wants that she cannot see what is right under her nose.

But it takes a certain kind of chauvinistic arrogance to believe that everything which has merit can be found wherever it is you come from. Perhaps the fundamentals of life are the same everywhere: people have friends and family the world over. But if you are hungry for all that life has to offer, you are not going to be satiated if you restrict your cultural diet to local produce.

Even if the ultimate prize is to be won at home, that doesn't mean travel is not worthwhile. As T. S. Eliot wrote, 'We shall not cease from exploration, and the end of all our exploring will be to arrive where we started and know the place for the first time.' Without exploration, the place we start from remains unknown. Travel need not divert us from valuing home, but make us appreciate it more fully.

Compare and contrast

Travel broadens the mind. *Early 20th century*

The nest is enough for a wren. *Irish proverb*

They change the clime, not their frame of mind, who rush across the sea. *Horace (65–8 BCE)*

75. A man is known by the company he keeps

Mid 16th century

'You can tell a lot about a person from their shoes,' a friend once said to me. I guffawed disdainfully, but in retrospect, perhaps I was a little harsh.

There is a sense in which anything and everything about any part of us might reveal something interesting or important about our whole. If Jean-Paul Sartre is right and 'You are nothing other than your life,' then there is no pure core of self behind our actions – the self is just all that we do, including choosing shoes.

Even so, shoes alone provide ambiguous and insufficient information. A shabby old pair might indicate poverty, wilful neglect or a temporary emergency measure. Likewise, a pair of Jimmy Choos might be indicative of an aspirational lifestyle, a particular fondness for shoes or simply the existence of a fashionable gift-giving relative. Your shoes say something about you, but their utterances are incomplete.

The same could be said for a better marker of who we are: the company we keep. Few things reflect our values better than whom we choose to spend our time with. But there is no simple way of reading off character traits from the qualities of friends and acquaintances. Some people hold a special place in our hearts for very idiosyncratic reasons. You may in general, for example, have no time for Tory Catholic dipsomaniacs, but one person who meets that description may also be the one person in the world who also appreciates the precise comic talents you love in Terry Scott. Things that would ordinarily irritate you are forgiven for the joy of bonding over old DVDs of *Terry and June* and *DangerMouse*.

Such complications are routinely ignored. People jump to conclusions about others on the basis of what they wear and whom they know. If such signals meant nothing at all, it is unlikely they would ever have come to be used as such short cuts. But if they meant as much as they are often assumed to, we would not be the strange and complicated creatures we evidently are.

Compare and contrast

Love me, love my dog. *Early 16th century*

Tell me with whom he mixes and I'll tell you who he is. *Spanish proverb*

He who sleeps with dogs wakes up with fleas. *French proverb*

76. Regret for the things we did can be tempered by time; it is regret for the things we did not do that is inconsolable

Sidney J. Harris (1917–86)

If you're not sure how to cast your vote in an election, or whether to order *tarte tatin* or tiramisu, being told that 'you'll regret what you don't do' is no help at all. Yet the same saying is often applied to people considering moving overseas, running away with lovers or starting a new business, as a reason to 'go for it'. What strange kind of advice are we dealing with here?

The answer is that it is not advice at all. Believing that we will regret what we *don't* do cannot help us decide what we *should* do, for the simple reason that anything we do leaves some other possibilities undone. If tempted by infidelity, for example, you will end up either not remaining faithful or not having the affair. Britons could regret adopting the Euro or not adopting it. Either way there is always something you didn't do to regret.

The mistake people make is to confuse what is in fact an insight into a tragic feature of human life and psychology with advice. For the wisdom in Harris's words is that whatever we do, we will wonder what would have happened if we had gone down another route. And whereas we have to live with the downsides of the choices we make, we tend to think only of the upsides of those options we rejected.

The irony is that Harris's saying is invoked most often by those afraid of missing out on life's experiences. But while it is true that timidity and fear of the unknown can prevent us from doing many worthwhile things, the core truth these words reflect is that we cannot go down every path open to us and what we don't do becomes a ghostly absence that follows in the shadow of the one life we actually carve out for ourselves.

Compare and contrast

Thinking first is an asset, regret later is useless. *Indonesian proverb*

Youth is a blunder; Manhood a struggle; Old age a regret. *Benjamin Disraeli (1804–81)*

Regret is an appalling waste of energy; you can't build on it; it's only good for wallowing in. *Katherine Mansfield (1888–1923)*

77. When one door shuts, another opens

Late 16th century

We hear much about the power of positive thinking today. Some go so far as to say that it is the secret power which brings some success which eludes others. If you want something enough, and ask the universe for it, it will happen.

This is a monstrous lie. How many people have wanted and begged whatever higher power there might be to stop their loved ones dying, with silence the only response? Is it a greater desire and focus which enables some babies to emerge into the world with silver spoons in their mouths while others die of malnutrition? Should the finger of blame be pointed at those who have failed, saying, 'You just didn't want it enough'?

Such ways of thinking have led people to take quite literally Hamlet's line that 'There is nothing either good or bad, but thinking makes it so.' If every exit is an entrance, and every problem an opportunity, then it seems everything that is bad in life is also really good.

This Panglossian outlook is surely not what any sane person would assent to on reflection. Even if every obstacle is an opportunity, that does not mean that it isn't a very real obstacle nonetheless. It is not that the bad is really good, but that even from the bad, some good can come.

If those goods are sufficiently valuable, we may even be glad of the suffering that led us to them. But that is not true of all opportunities which open up only because things are not right in the first place. For instance, we would not have the chance to embrace hope if we never confronted the possibility of despair. But often it would have been better not to have faced the despair in the first place.

Rather than providing glib reassurance, the thought that every obstacle is an opportunity should lead us to look squarely at the obstacle for what it is and not wish it were something more benign. The surest way out of a hole has to be found from within it, not by imagining it's not really a hole at all.

Compare and contrast

One person's death is another's bread. *Dutch proverb*

Every obstacle is an opportunity. *Italian proverb*

Everyone makes lumber from a fallen tree. *Spanish proverb*

78. A prophet has no honour in his own country

John 4:43

Given the adoration poured on him by some of his acolytes, it is not entirely incongruous that this expression applied as much to the late Jacques Derrida as it did to Jesus. Despite having a reputation as the embodiment of French intellectual pretension and obscurity at its worst, Derrida was always more popular abroad than he was at home. Ironically, given the cultural gulf between France and America, Derrida's reputation as a leading world intellectual was built more than anywhere else in the United States.

Yet it would be very odd to cite this as evidence that Derrida was as good as his supporters claim. The mere fact that foreigners love you is no proof of your greatness. If you have any doubts about that, just remember that in 1989 David Hasselhoff was named 'Most Popular and Best Selling Artist of the Year' in Germany.

A similar twisted logic also provides comfort to those who fail to achieve the success they crave in any territory. Van Gogh's genius was never recognized in his lifetime, we tell ourselves, hopeful that posterity will judge us more kindly than our contemporaries. But for every genius discovered late, there are thousands of would-be geniuses whom history judges as harshly as their peers.

It is a logical nonsense to conclude that, since a prophet has no honour in his own country, and I have no honour in my country, therefore I am a prophet. Yet the fallacy is seductive, especially when implicitly reasoned rather than explicitly set out. But you may as well argue that cats have no flippers, and I have no flippers, therefore I must be a cat.

It may be true that a prophet has no honour in his country, but then nor does a tax collector. Just as fame is no guarantee of quality, lack of fame is no hallmark of excellence. Obscurity is usually the only thing we have in common with unsung talents.

Compare and contrast

No man is a hero to his valet. *Mme Cornuel (1605–94)*

Every man has a lurking wish to appear considerable in his native place. *Samuel Johnson (1709–84)*

I should one day like to show by my work what such an eccentric, such a nobody, has in his heart. *Vincent van Gogh (1853–90)*

79. A trouble shared is a trouble halved

Mid 20th century

If you have a problem, there is convincing evidence that simply talking about it will cut it down to size. Research on psychotherapeutic 'talking cures', for example, shows that people with problems feel better when given some sort of listening-based, supportive environment in which to discuss their problems, and not only when these are with trained therapists, although actual therapy has better results than such 'placebos'.[8]

Why this should be so is not clear. Common sense talks of the benefits of 'getting it off your chest', but it may be that simply giving a name to a problem helps us to deal with it. Psychologist Matthew D. Lieberman has used brain imaging techniques to identify what happens when we label emotions. The critical area is the amygdala, which serves as a kind of alarm system. When you see an angry face, for example, even if it is too quickly for it to register consciously, the amygdala increases its activity. However, when you simply label a face as 'angry', that decreases the amygdala's activity. This seems to have something to do with the right ventrolateral prefrontal cortex, which helps us to control emotion.

The science may be technical and difficult, but in practice, the message is clear. 'In the same way you hit the brake when you're driving when you see a yellow light,' says Lieberman, 'when you put your feelings into words, you seem to be hitting the brakes on your emotional response.'

However, there is not yet any research that shows that listening to the problems of others makes the hearer feel better. Sharing a problem may half the sharer's slice, but it may not make the whole pie any smaller. What's worse, the benefits of sharing do not multiply each time it happens. Lieberman's brake metaphor is telling: most of the benefit occurs when you first apply it. In other words, persistent and repeated problem sharers may actually be spreading and multiplying the misery, not reducing it.

Compare and contrast

Many hands make light work. *Mid 14th century*

Shared grief is half grief. *Dutch proverb*

A misfortune shared is half a joy. *Italian proverb*

80. Death is nothing to us, since when we are, death has not come, and when death has come, we are not

Epicurus (341–270 BCE)

As long as there have been philosophers, there has been some bafflement as to why we are so worried about death. After all, we don't wake up in the small hours of the morning filled with dread at the thought of what it was like *before* we existed. So why worry ourselves with what will happen after? If not existing is something we could happily not live with once, we can easily not live with it again. In death nothing either good or bad can happen to us, so we have literally nothing to worry about.

Yet very few of us face the prospect of extinction with complete equanimity. Indeed, the person who doesn't mind at all whether she lives or dies is usually considered mentally disturbed, not at peace with the eternal truths of mortality.

So are we just idiots who cannot see the obvious facts Epicurus et al. have pointed out? Not at all. It is not just that if you believe there may be an avenging God, some apprehension about the state of death is entirely rational. Nor that it is hard to disentangle how much our fear is of dying, rather than death itself.

To be alive is to have plans, desires, attachments, projects and friends. Because we care about such things, of course the prospect of them not being there will distress us. That need not be based on any false idea that once dead we will miss them, but merely on the present desire that they continue to exist. To want not to be dead is simply the logical concomitant of the desire to be alive and enjoy all that life offers us. It is the very fact that death is nothing, and life is a sometimes wonderful something, that makes death matter to we who will never experience it.

Compare and contrast

Death will find me alive. *Italian proverb*

It matters not how a man dies, but how he lives. *Samuel Johnson (1709–84)*

It's not that I'm afraid to die. I just don't want to be there when it happens. *Woody Allen (1935–)*

81. To the pessimist, the glass is half-empty. To the optimist, it is half-full

20th century

Do you see the glass as half-empty of half-full? 'It depends on whether you're pouring or drinking,' says Bill Cosby. Neither, says George Carlin. 'I see a glass that's twice as big as it needs to be.' 'Who cares?' say countless internet jokers, 'Just drink it.'

The gags accentuate the central point of the saying, which is that there is always more than one way to see a situation. Nor is perspective simply a matter of seeing facts differently, it is also about the attitude one chooses to adopt: optimistic, pessimistic, ironic or dismissive.

It's easy to make too much of this benign relativism. The fact that there is a choice of descriptors does not mean that there are no objective facts. You can see a pint glass as half-empty or half-full, but there is only one correct answer as to how much liquid it contains: 284ml. Much depends on perspective, but a great deal does not.

Sometimes, it is not a question of perspective, but context. Cosby's joke illustrates this well: when you're in the middle of pouring a drink it is halfway to being full, when in the middle of drinking it, it's halfway to being empty. This isn't a matter of how you choose to see it, but a matter of how things really are.

The reason the half-full/half-empty glass question is quite a good test for optimism and pessimism is that it works by stripping away context to probe what your default setting is: to perceive what you don't have or what you do. But in real life, there is always a context, and so it is not always a simple matter of choice as to how you see things. Different descriptions may not be simply right or wrong, but they can be better or worse.

Not every situation that requires judgement is comparable to the half-empty glass. Rather, we need the serenity to accept the things that just are, the imagination to see things which could be viewed differently, and the wisdom to know the difference between the two.

Compare and contrast

Half a loaf is better than no bread. *Mid 16th century*

Every cloud has a silver lining. *Mid 19th century*

Better one-eyed than blind. *German proverb*

82. Have nothing in your houses that you do not know to be useful or believe to be beautiful

William Morris (1834–96)

As I write this, I am sitting in a small, cluttered room which I have been intending to 'sort out' for months. How might the advice of William Morris, designer, writer and socialist, help me decide what to do about it?

First, I suppose I should get rid of everything I know not to be useful. The trouble is that 90 per cent of all clutter comprises things we know could be useful one day, such as the two packs of computer screen wipes, a light bulb, a travel plug adaptor, and a rarely used fax machine, all of which are making my room look untidy.

Second, there are some things that are not useful, such as the painting by an asylum seeker of military helicopters over Mogadishu, and a print of Joseph Wright of Derby's asphyxiating dove in an air pump. Perhaps I can keep them, if we say that Morris really should have said 'of aesthetic merit' rather than 'beautiful'.

A few things remain that still break his rule. I have one or two small boxes which I label 'Unchuckable Misc.' as well as some photo albums. I'm not one for accumulating large amounts of memorabilia, but there are some things from my past life which I would like to keep. Most are neither useful nor beautiful.

So Morris's advice turns out to be a combination of the incomplete and the obvious. For who would want to keep anything they neither thought had a use or did not like? And why should we get rid of things which fit neither description but have some value, sentimental or financial?

I often hear Morris's words quoted favourably by people who claim to follow his maxim. However, his advice is usually heeded only to the extent that it is what we do anyway, and ignored to the extent that it is far too narrow. If you want to truly transform your home, any old TV makeover show is probably going to give you more concrete guidance than Morris's vague and vacuous precept.

Compare and contrast

The worth of a thing is what it will bring. *Mid 16th century*

A thing of beauty is a joy forever. *John Keats (1795–1821)*

Remember that the most beautiful things in the world are the most useless; peacocks and lilies, for instance. *John Ruskin (1819–1900)*

83. Better safe than sorry

Mid 19th century

Network Rail, the Chief Fire Officers Association, the mining multinational Rio Tinto, British Nuclear Fuels and British Airways, along with countless other public and private bodies, have all proudly claimed that 'safety is our first priority'. There's nothing surprising in that. Can you imagine, say, Virgin trains announcing that safety was their *second* priority, behind comfort, convenience or creating amusing photo opportunities for Richard Branson?

But although it is politically and commercially difficult to say that time and money which could be spent on making something safer should be directed elsewhere, sometimes, that's just what we should say. Most obviously, we may refuse to use our resources to reduce a specific danger because spending the same amount on other alternatives will increase overall safety. For example, after the 1999 Ladbroke Grove train disaster in London, it was estimated that the billions of pounds spent on a proposed rail safety scheme would have saved up to 500 times more lives if spent on the roads.

More fundamentally, unless we want to spend all our money on protecting ourselves, at some point we will opt to use our cash for things other than safety. Every pound spent on the arts, for example, could have gone into public health or safety. And what is true for money is also true for time and energy. You could always spend a bit longer checking your car is safe, testing your electrical appliances or even monitoring your tap water purity.

If safety concerns become too dominant, you cease being better safe than sorry and become both safe *and* sorry. There is more than one road to regret, and though misery caused by a failure to take precautions is particularly hard to take, the loss and longing caused by a failure to take any risks at all can be just as painful and more insidious. Caution can actually cause sorrow, so just because it may always be better to be safe than sorry, that doesn't mean it is always better to be safe.

Compare and contrast

He who fights and runs away, may live to fight another day. *Mid 16th century*

Prudence is the mother of safety. *French proverb*

Let water you don't need to drink flow. *Spanish proverb*

84. The best lack all convictions, while the worst are full of passionate intensity

W. B. Yeats (1865–1939)

Ireland's sectarian hatreds provided the inspiration for Yeats's famous lines in *The Second Coming*, but suicide bombers, brutal left- and right-wing ideologues, religious zealots or fiery nationalists could all have been equal to the task. While it is not difficult to think of people who committed terrible atrocities thanks to an intensity of commitment to a cause, no carnage has been created by hordes of the apathetic and indifferent. You can't rouse a mob with the cry 'What do we want?' when the reply is 'we don't really know' and 'we don't rightly care'.

However, it would be a mistake to interpret Yeats's insightful observation for an endorsement of apathy. It is one thing to *describe*, quite another to *prescribe*. The fact that 'passionate intensity' is the preserve of the worst can be as much a lament as a caution. For when only the bad have a fire in their bellies, the bad will prevail. Hence Burke's claim that 'All that is necessary for evil to succeed is that good men do nothing.' If the best lack all convictions, they leave the path clear for the bad to do their worst.

The message to the good is therefore twofold: if they are serious about wanting good to triumph, they need to weaken the convictions of the bad or gain a bit more passion themselves.

The message could not be more timely, as Western democratic liberalism struggles with the challenge of extremism from Christian, Islamic and nationalist minorities. It is just not enough to trust our own decency. We need to win the argument against fanaticism or, failing that, be prepared to defend our values with a bit more of the passionate intensity we see in our foes. Otherwise, we face the prospect described by Yeats, where 'Things fall apart; the centre cannot hold / Mere anarchy is loosed upon the world / The blood-dimmed tide is loosed, and everywhere / The ceremony of innocence is drowned'.

Compare and contrast

If a man will begin with certainties, he shall end in doubts; but if he will be content to begin with doubts, he shall end in certainties. *Francis Bacon (1561–1626)*

There lives more faith in honest doubt / Believe me, than in half the creeds. *Alfred, Lord Tennyson (1809–92)*

The passion is the measure of the holder's lack of rational conviction. *Bertrand Russell (1872–1970)*

85. Let sleeping dogs lie

Late 14th century

One of the most popular ways in which quotes and phrases live today is as inspirational messages, on posters, fridge magnets or daily emails. This is something of an aberration, because a large proportion of traditional sayings are not encouragements to act, but warnings against doing anything.

One such cluster gathers around the various ways in which it is better to avoid difficult situations than deal with them: don't rock the boat; people in glass houses shouldn't throw stones; and let sleeping dogs lie.

In each of these three cases, the imagery is striking and often apt. We are often in fragile or precarious situations where rashness is the greatest danger. Indeed, one of the best arguments against any kind of 'optional war' is that the perils of induced anarchy are often greater than those of settled despotism.

However, the question of what to do with a potentially troublesome hound deserves a better answer than simply to leave it alone. Everything depends on what is likely to happen when the beast awakes. If you'll be long gone by then, then tip-toeing past is probably the best option. But if you really have to do something with your dog, it might be better to do it while it's calm, if not actually unconscious, than wait until it is running around chasing rabbits.

Most people quite understandably do not like dealing with difficult problems and will seek any excuse to put off confronting them. This means the biggest issues are dealt with only when people 'reach rock bottom' or a 'crisis point'. It would be so much better if we could sort out our gravest difficulties when things are at their least, not most, tumultuous.

Far from being too keen to stir sleeping animals, our problem is usually that we are all too inclined to pretend that temporary tranquillity is an indicator that nothing needs to be done. To mix metaphors, if you have to grab the bull by the horns, better to do it when it's dreaming than when it's charging towards you.

Compare and contrast

Never trouble trouble till trouble troubles you. *Late 19th century*

Don't wake the cat that sleeps. *French proverb*

Don't wake the bear that sleeps. *Swedish proverb*

86. The course of true love never did run smooth

William Shakespeare (1564–1616)

Most popular songs can be divided into two categories: those which are about the joys of love and those which are about its pains. For every 'I Want to Hold your Hand', there's a 'Yesterday'.

We could glibly talk about the yin and the yang, but simply recognizing that, as Lynn Anderson sang, 'Along with the sunshine, there's gotta be a little rain sometimes,' doesn't get us very far. Consider for example, a musical conversation between Anderson and Neil Diamond, in which Neil sings 'You don't bring me flowers, you don't sing me love songs. You hardly talk to me any more when you come through the door.' Would it be good enough for Anderson to reply, 'I beg your pardon, I never promised you a rose garden'?

The problem is that the course of false love is not exactly even either. Being told that true love's path is stony can therefore provide false reassurance to those heading in the wrong direction just as easily as it can fortify the hearts of true lovers in stormy waters.

Fundamentally, it is life which is difficult, not love especially. That is why the wedding vows are right to make two people who decide to live as one agree to do so for better and for worse, in sickness and in health.

Life's inherent imperfection means that even the best-matched couples are likely to face obstacles. Lysander, who warns about the course of love in Act I of *A Midsummer Night's Dream*, lists some such problems: 'either it was different in blood; or else misgraffed in respect of years; or else it stood upon the choice of friends. If there were a sympathy in choice, war, death, or sickness did lay siege to it, making it momentary as a sound, swift as a shadow, short as any dream.'

It is the course of love which is uneven, not true love itself. So when relationships are bad, we have to ask whether the problem is with the path or the travellers.

Compare and contrast

The quarrel of lovers is the renewal of love. *Early 16th century*

A deaf husband and a blind wife are always a happy couple. *Late 16th century*

Who loves us well will make us cry. *Spanish proverb*

87. *In vino veritas*

Pliny the Elder (AD 23–79)

If you are trying to suppress rage, anger or hatred, inebriation is not recommended. Many a divorce has been precipitated by a drunken admission of love lost, or found elsewhere. In such situations, it is natural to think that alcohol is a truth drug.

Harsh words, however, are not the greatest risk of imbibing. In Britain, 60–70 per cent of murders, nearly half of all violent crimes, and over a third of all domestic assaults are believed to be committed under the influence. If alcohol simply reveals the truth, then it seems sobriety is little more than a constant repression of violent urges.

This grim conclusion can be avoided if we distinguish between two of alcohol's effects. First of all it is a disinhibitor. This means that what we ordinarily find it hard to say or do becomes much easier after a drink or three.

But alcohol also has another set of effects. Under its influence, the functioning of the cerebral cortex becomes impaired while the limbic system takes greater control. That means emotions take priority over reasoning, and more instinctive reactions and drives, like fight-or-flight and sexual desire, come to the fore.

What this means is that when we are drunk, it is not just that our normal desires and feelings are unchained, we actually have thoughts and desires that we do not usually have at all, or to a much lesser extent. For example, what would normally be a mild awareness of someone's attractiveness becomes a fiercer desire for sexual congress.

This is why *in vino veritas* is not quite right. What we say and do when drunk does not always reflect what we'd like to say and do when sober. This is the tragedy of many a drunken murder or suicide: the violent action is not one the perpetrator really wanted at all. The fact that there is often a pre-existing desire waiting for the alcohol to magnify does not mean that the drunken version of it is its most authentic manifestation. The idea that we are more fully ourselves when drunk is not a wise insight, but a common delusion of the dipsomaniac.

Compare and contrast

When the wine is in, the wit is out. *Late 14th century*

The drunk and children tell the truth. *German proverb*

What you wish for when you're sober, you act out when drunk. *Greek proverb*

88. The only thing we have to fear is fear itself

Franklin D. Roosevelt (1882–1945)

'When I go out to dinner, there's nothing to wear but clothes,' sang Louis Jordan in 'Life Is So Peculiar', adding such other comic insights as 'Whenever I get thirsty, there's nothing to do but drink.' He might have added, 'Whenever something's scary, there's nothing to feel but fear.'

Roosevelt's famous line can sound similarly tautological. That it is not can be seen by returning to the occasion of its first utterance, the inaugural presidential address of 4 March 1933. America was in the depths of the Great Depression. This, and nothing else, was what he and his audience were thinking about when he issued his call to defy fear. What he said was, 'Let me assert my firm belief that the only thing we have to fear is fear itself – nameless, unreasoning, unjustified terror which paralyses needed efforts to convert retreat into advance.'

What Roosevelt believed was that the fear of the American people in the Depression had taken on a life of its own. It was born out of a real crisis, a real danger, but after the initial crash, in the midst of a long economic slump, the object of fear had vanished into the past, while the feeling of fear still remained, detached. Hence Roosevelt was not making a general claim about the nature of fear, he was diagnosing a particular pathology, the 'unreasoning, unjustified terror' of his age.

That is not to say his words are so rooted to their original time and place that they hold no use for us now. All we need to remember is that they are not universally true. Sometimes there really is something to be afraid of. But often, like a child unable to go to sleep after a nightmare, fear lingers long after the reason for it has disappeared. In such situations, and only in such situations, should Roosevelt's words return to fortify our resolve.

Compare and contrast

Cowards may die many times before their death. *Late 16th century*

Fear lends wings. *German proverb*

Better be killed than frightened to death. *R. S. Surtees (1803–64)*

89. Do to others what you would have them do to you

Matthew 7:12

From the golden rule of Confucius to the categorical imperative of Kant, through the Hindu rule of dharma, all the major moral systems in history have stressed the importance of doing unto others as you would be done by. The principle is such a commonplace that it can seem obviously right. But taken too literally it is even more obviously wrong.

The problem is that a fully developed moral sense requires an awareness of the difference of others as well as their sameness. For example, praise which would please one person will embarrass another. While we may prefer always to be told the truth, others may prefer it if we didn't voice our negative or critical opinions about them.

Gift-giving provides a further example of how a failure to see the world from another's point of view can lead to offence and upset. Giving unto others what we would have them give us is a recipe for discontent. What would delight us as a generous, luxury offering might strike another as a frivolous waste of time and money. And giving a gift which is to your taste, but not that of the recipient, can imply a condescending criticism of the things they value.

We are right to take offence at such gifts, because they show a failure to follow the true spirit of the golden rule.

What is good is not treating everyone in exactly the same way, but treating people with the same respect that we expect from them. This is a respect for the unique worth of each life and the freedom to live as we see fit within reasonable limits. But we can't show this respect if we do not even recognize what makes their lives particular and how their choices may differ from our own. That is why what we actually do can, and often should, differ according to who we are doing it to.

Compare and contrast

One should never do that to another which one regards as injurious to one's own self. *The Mahabharata*

Never impose on others what you would not choose for yourself. *Confucius (551–479 BCE)*

Act only according to that maxim whereby you can at the same time will that it should become a universal law. *Immanuel Kant (1724–1804)*

90. When in Rome, do as the Romans do

Late 15th century

'It involves Russia.' Woody Allen's distillation of *War and Peace* is an extreme example of how much which is crucial is often lost in summary. So it is with the saying, 'When in Rome . . .', which is a paraphrase of a more complete piece of advice from St Ambrose, penned back in the 4th century.

The good saint had noted that the churches in Milan and Rome fasted on different days of the week. He counselled others to 'follow the custom of whatever church you attend, if you do not want to give or receive scandal'.

This is obviously a much more cautious policy than simply copying everything the Romans do, which is understandable, for no devout Christian could in good conscience mimic the kind of depravity found in parts of any major metropolis.

Even without an ecclesiastical motivation for refusing to throw ourselves into every local custom we come across, there are reasons for taking Ambrose's advice in its original spirit. For surely it is neither moral nor prudent to copy uncritically every practice of the lands we visit. Multinational corporations, for example, often work in countries where bribery is endemic. Yet we fully expect their officials not to adopt these local conventions in the name of cultural experimentation and respect for difference. Never does the phrase 'When in Rome . . .' ring more hollow than when it is used to justify manifest wrongdoing on the grounds that it's just what everyone else is doing. St Ambrose never intended his advice to go that far, and in that respect we should remain true to his intentions.

Caution is advisable for hedonistic as well as ethical reasons. When actually in Rome, many travellers will boldly tuck into local delicacies such as tripe or rigatoni with baby veal's intestines. But when in the US, these gourmands do not mimic the local penchant for mall food halls and fast-food joints. Every rule has its exceptions.

Compare and contrast

With the wolves one must howl. *German proverb*

Wherever you go, do as you see. *Spanish proverb*

Only dead fish swim with the stream. *Malcolm Muggeridge (1903–90)*

91. Boys will be boys

Early 17th century

Not so long ago the phrase 'boys' toys' would have brought to mind Lego, train sets and plastic guns. Now, as websites like boystoys.co.uk and bigboystoyz.com testify, it means gadgets and games for grown men, like mini remote-control battle helicopters, USB missile launchers or the Gentleman's Ball Scratcher 'for the days when your own hands are just not precise enough'.

The phrase 'boys will be boys' has similarly expanded its age range, so that it no longer mostly explains the exuberant excesses of children, but mainly excuses the peccadilloes of adults. It represents the death of the spirit of St Paul, who wrote, 'When I became a man, I put away childish things.' If boys will be boys, and men are still boys, then men are excused the responsibility of having to improve their behaviour to reflect their apparently mature status.

However, generational blurring is not the main reason why 'boys will be boys' has become problematic. Its wide use reflects a backlash against the kind of feminism that asserted that gender differences are essentially social constructs. This view has become widely discredited, in part due to resistance from precisely those conservative social forces feminists warned about, but also because of the weight of evidence from neuroscience and psychology that there are indeed numerous average differences between male and female patterns of thought and feeling. Claims that men are from Mars and that women can't read maps have passed from old-dated lore to scientifically supported truisms in one generation.

But to conclude that it is therefore no use complaining about gender roles is to draw more from the science than is warranted. The fact that there are biologically determined average differences between male and female brains does not mean that all actual differences observed in men and women in particular societies are natural and unchangeable. Indeed, it should be obvious that gender roles are very malleable, as the large amount of child-rearing by men in Scandinavia and the absence of women drivers in Saudi Arabia illustrate.

As is so often the case, there is no stark choice between nature and nurture: both have their part to play. Boys will be boys, but men still have more freedom to behave differently from how they do than too many would care to admit.

Compare and contrast

Wanton kittens make sober cats. *Early 18th century*

Little fish will grow big. *French proverb*

The child is the father of the man. *William Wordsworth (1770–1850)*

92. Genius is one per cent inspiration, ninety-nine per cent perspiration

Thomas Edison (1847–1931)

Statistical analogies suffer from the same weakness as actual statistics: they may not lie, but they sure can mislead. For instance, when quality not quantity is the issue, 1 per cent can make all the difference.

Consider human DNA. Most scientists agree that humans share about 98.5 percent of our genetic code with chimpanzees. However, it would be very misleading to say that humans are therefore 98.5 per cent chimp. After all, we share 50 per cent of our DNA with bananas, but that doesn't make us half-human, half-plantain. What makes each kind of biological organism unique is determined by their small genetic differences, not their numerically greater similarities.

What is literally true of DNA is metaphorically true of genius. Edison's analogy is often taken to mean that we can all be brilliant if we work hard enough. But just as the 1 per cent difference between our DNA and that of our closest primate relatives is enough to ensure that a chimp can never be a human, so the 1 per cent of exceptional talent that the genius mixes with her sweat is enough to set her apart from even the most industrious of the less gifted. Sheer hard work can take you closer to genius, but it can't earn you the cigar.

However, such stark realism about the limitations of our abilities is out of tune with our egalitarian, democratic times, in which someone such as Arnold Schwarzenegger profits at election time by populist rhetoric such as 'You can achieve anything' as long as you 'work hard'.

Edison's words are most useful not for the majority striving for greatness, but for geniuses mindful of what they need to do to exploit their gifts. Still, the 99 per cent perspiration they need to fulfil their potential is theirs to sweat out. The 1 per cent of inspiration the rest of us lack will always elude us.

Compare and contrast

Genius is an infinite capacity for taking pains. *Late 19th century*

Genius without education is like silver in the mine. *American proverb*

A steady drop will carve the stone. *German proverb*

93. More tears are shed over answered prayers than unanswered ones

Truman Capote (1924–84)

'A dream come true' is just about the most enthusiastic description of an experience or state of affairs that you can get, topped only by 'better than my wildest dreams'. Yet there is also a recurring idea that getting what you want is the last thing you should want. As George Bernard Shaw put it, 'There are two tragedies in life. One is not to get your heart's desire. The other is to get it.' So where's the truth? Are there no such things as dreams, only nightmares we haven't got to the end of?

It is certainly true that the reality of what we aspire to often disappoints. There is an unfortunate tendency to think that some future achievement will be our salvation. If only we had this, or did that, *then* we'd be complete. If we think in this way it is indeed better to travel hopefully than to arrive, for although at some point we are all finished, we're never completed. Capote was right about one thing: the disappointment of discovering your values and ideals are empty can be more crushing than the frustration of never truly realizing them.

It is also true that we often don't think through the consequences of our ambitions. People buy idyllic country cottages, only to realize they hate being isolated and twenty miles from the nearest source of food and drink. Others get where they want in their careers, but underestimate the cost to their personal lives and states of mind. We think we know what we want when we should know that our desires are only as reliable as the beliefs that inform them.

Neither of these dispiriting truths, however, is a good reason not to dream. Rather, they are reminders that our dreams must be lucid. As the saying goes, 'Be careful what you wish for', not 'don't wish for anything at all'. With the wrong aspirations, life is like swimming hard in the wrong direction. But without any aspiration at all, we are simply treading water.

Compare and contrast

Be careful what you wish for, you might just get it. *Early 20th century*

Grandma gave a dinar to dance, and two to stop. *Bosnian proverb*

If men had all they wished, they would be often ruined. *Aesop (620–560 BCE)*

94. To know all is to forgive all

Mid 20th century

After the London suicide bombings of July 2005, people struggled to understand how four outwardly good, decent people could have killed themselves deliberately, in order to slaughter others indiscriminately. Yet if we do not understand what leads people to such barbarous acts, how can we have any hope of stopping others following in their wake?

At the same time, people are reluctant to understand too much. *Tout comprendre c'est tout pardoner*, as the French say: to understand all is to forgive all. Justice, however, requires that we do not pardon all, which is what we fear will happen if we are too understanding of criminal acts.

Consider how Bashir Ahmed, the uncle of suicide bomber Shezhad Tanweer, was criticized for saying that his nephew was 'looking for justice'. Even though Ahmed clearly thought the bombings were wrong, the mere suggestion that Tanweer's motivation could have been principled from his point of view was too much for some. The *News of the World*, for example, condemned Ahmed for offering a 'perverse justification for the atrocity'.

But to explain is not the same as to excuse or justify. All Bashir Ahmed did was to describe his nephew's sense of grievance. You could even accept the legitimacy of the grievance without in any way excusing the atrocities carried out in its name.

True, it is hard to maintain a crude distinction between the righteous and the wicked if you do fully understand why people do terrible things. But tough justice does not require black and white morality. Wrongdoing must be resisted, whether it is perpetrated by devils or flawed human beings.

It is absurd to suggest that if we did fully understand the minds of suicide bombers, we would no longer want to stop them, or would even join them ourselves. All we have to lose from greater understanding is just the same kind of dangerous arrogance of absolute moral certainty that leads others to slaughter innocents.

Compare and contrast

There is, however, a limit at which forbearance ceases to be a virtue. *Edmund Burke (1729–97)*

Total understanding makes one very indulgent. *Madame de Staël (1766–1817)*

Tolerance is only another name for indifference. *W. Somerset Maugham (1874–1965)*

95. A man reaps what he sows

Galatians 6:7

To seek order in an apparently chaotic world is only human. Sometimes that search reveals regularities that are really there, as is the case in science. Some other patterns we discern, such as those in astrology and numerology, are just the product of wishful or bad thinking.

One of the many things we would like to be regulated by natural laws is justice. It seems intolerable that bad things happen to good people, or – perhaps even worse – good things happen to bad people. We seem to find these injustices deeply offensive, which is why we would rather believe they are merely apparent, and not real.

We can do this by believing in one version or other of the karmic principle that 'what goes around, comes around'. Shit happens, but in the end, the chickens will come home to roost, and the meek shall inherit the earth.

It's a reassuring theory, but it can be made to fit the evidence only if we believe in an afterlife, or previous lives, because on this earth people quite evidently don't always get their just deserts.

Perhaps more important is how this way of thinking affects our reaction to misfortune. Although a sense of justice may sow the seeds of the idea, when reaped it has a more poisonous edge. When Michael Portillo lost his seat in 1997, the Twin Towers fell in New York, and people died from BSE, sympathy for the victims was often tainted by a kind of *Schadenfreude,* provoked by the thought that a person, a country or modern farming was being paid back for past wrongs.

Even worse is that the reap-what-you-sow doctrine encourages the belief that if someone is suffering, it must be their fault. Believing that the natural order of things will take care of justice, far from being a moral position, is perhaps only a means of salving our consciences and removing the imperative for human sympathy.

Compare and contrast

To every pig comes its sabbath. *Spanish proverb*

What you do you must expect. *Italian proverb*

What one dishes out, he must also eat. *German proverb*

96. The grass is always greener on the other side of the fence

Mid 20th century

As Britain becomes a more urban, consumerist society, the rural image of green fields and fences seems an increasingly quaint way to represent envy and aspiration. Our green fields are the light-wood fittings and white walls of Scandinavian urban chic, and the fences we consider scrambling over are only as high as our credit cards.

The incongruity of the natural setting aside, the expression rings truer than ever. But just as paranoia is no guarantee that they're not out to get us, so recognition of the dangers of idealizing alternative lives does not mean that some adjoining fields really aren't more lush.

Some of the people who know this best are people who, in retrospect, took too long to leave their lovers. It seems to be a very common experience for women in particular to stay in relationships that are bad for them way beyond their sell-by date. One reason why they do is that they tell themselves – and are often told by others – that they should be satisfied with what they've got. To push the metaphor further than it can perhaps go, their small enclosure may be cramped and muddy compared to the open fields of singledom, but at least it contains a tame bullock in reasonable condition.

Only after they have plucked up the courage and left do

they realize that, on this occasion at least, they really have been grazing on inadequate pastures for too long. These women aren't stupid. What they show is how hard it is to apply the wisdom of the metaphor. We all know we tend to idealize what we don't have and that this should make us think twice about whether we should make radical changes. But when we come to think thrice, precisely how much we need to correct for the distortion of rose-tinted spectacles is as unclear as ever.

Compare and contrast

The other is liked more for being other than good. *Spanish proverb*

Someone else's rice cake always looks bigger. *Korean proverb*

Cattle in faraway lands have long horns. *Irish proverb*

97. A rose by any other name would smell as sweet

William Shakespeare (1564–1616)

Wouldn't it be wonderful to live in a world where names and labels didn't matter? But they do – and more profoundly than might be expected.

At the most basic level, it is sadly the case that people do judge things on the basis of their names. For example, David N. Figlio at the University of Florida has conducted research that suggests 'teachers may use a child's name as a signal of unobserved parental contributions to that child's education, and expect less from children with names that "sound" like they were given by uneducated parents'.[9] Anecdotal evidence accords with this. Think, for example, how comedy characters almost always have names that play to the prejudices of viewers.

You might think this is all even more reason to heed the words of Shakespeare in Act II of *Romeo and Juliet*. We may, unfortunately, place too much emphasis on names, but if we did not, we would discover a rose by any other name smells as sweet. Alas, it does not.

Perception turns out to be a very complex thing which is deeply affected by expectation. For instance, in experiments, drinkers have been found to enjoy wine more if they think it is expensive. The critical finding of this research is that these drinkers don't merely say or believe that the wine is better, to them it really tastes as though it is. The way in which we process taste and smell is heavily influenced by what we think. Hence, for example, people can be blindfolded and told that the chocolate ice-cream they are eating is straw-berry, or the red wine white, and it will taste to them as though it really is.

None of this means that there aren't real differences between good wine and bad, the smell of roses and the odour of manure. All it means is that the way we talk and think about things is not just incidental: it has the power to change our experiences of them.

Compare and contrast

Hard words break no bones. *Late 17th century*

It's better to lose an eye than to get a bad name. *Greek proverb*

He who wants to drown his dog says it has rabies. *French proverb*

98. We cannot command nature except by obeying her

Francis Bacon (1561–1626)

'History shows again and again how nature points up the folly of men.' These lyrics from a Blue Öyster Cult song are made no less true by the fact that they come from a song which contains the slightly less profound lines, 'Oh no, there goes Tokyo / Go go Godzilla!' That nature must not be defied is part of our folk wisdom, accepted by almost everyone from American metal bands to liberal social commentators.

The difficulty comes in understanding what it means to defy nature. For the strange thing is that among those who would claim to agree with Francis Bacon you'll find both environmentalists and their mortal enemies, the scientists developing genetically modified organisms (GMOs).

The reason for this is that scientists and environmentalists have a very different idea of what it means to go against nature. For the scientist, of course you need to 'obey' nature, because nothing can break the laws of nature and still work. So, for instance, GMOs do not defy nature. If they did, they'd have remained science fiction.

Thus scientists are in complete agreement with Bacon. They see their job as commanding nature – in the sense of trying to harness nature for our own benefit – and they achieve this goal by working within the limits of possibility prescribed by nature's laws.

Those who think scientists go too far with their manipulation of nature therefore cannot cite Bacon in support. They might think that we cannot or should not command nature as much as we do, or that obeying her really should mean leaving her more or less as she is. But these injunctions go way beyond the demand to work with nature rather than against her. They rather spring from a caution against hubris and the fear that we may be moving too far too fast. There may be some sense in that, but as an intellectually satisfying rationale for restraint, it's more Blue Öyster Cult than Francis Bacon.

Compare and contrast

You can drive out nature with a pitchfork but she keeps on coming back. *Mid 16th century*

Chase away the natural and it returns at a gallop. *French proverb*

All things are artificial, for nature is the art of God. *Thomas Browne (1605–82)*

99. Where there's life, there's hope

Mid 16th century

What makes human life worth living? Some maintain the sanctity of life, which is of value in and of itself. Others claim that life is good for what it allows us to do, and is not a good in itself. For instance, humans have a uniquely rich self-consciousness. If we lose this, as we do in permanent vegetative states, we may lack what makes our lives worth preserving.

The disagreement can be summed up in the idea that one side takes the distinction between truly living and merely existing to be of paramount importance, whereas the other thinks that even 'mere existence' is of incalculable worth.

This difference is deep and makes the views mutually incompatible. This can be seen in how each side would regard the idea that where there is life, there is hope. The key question is, hope for what? On the sanctity of life view, hope is primarily for more life, and only secondarily for a better one. As long as someone lives, they have what matters most. Hope's primary object is more of the same.

For opponents of this view, there are forms of human life which are not worth living. In such cases, we need to know whether there is hope of moving beyond mere existence, and what price this future will exact. Sometimes there just is no such hope: a permanent vegetative state offers no promise of a return to true human existence. Without enough hope, we may be justified in ceasing our efforts to sustain a life, or even in taking steps to end it. The hope of more such life is simply not enough.

So for neither party does the expression 'where there's life, there's hope' really go to the heart of the matter. You need to ask what the hope is for. If it is simply for more life, it is usually true. But if hope is for more than mere existence, it may sadly be absent. In both cases, we cannot avoid a return to the fundamental question of value: what in life is worth hoping for?

Compare and contrast

There is hope as long as your fishing-line is in the water. *Norwegian proverb*

Hope keeps alive. *French proverb*

Those declared dead live longer. *German proverb*

100. Knowledge comes, but wisdom lingers

Alfred, Lord Tennyson (1809–92)

Wisdom is an idea which comforts the ignorant. Most of us have to live with the fact that there are many others brighter and more knowledgeable than ourselves. These people have read, digested and memorized vast amounts of information, and many of them have powers of deduction and inference that work many times faster than our own. But, we ask ourselves, are they *wise*?

Wisdom is not mental agility or information retention, but a special kind of insight that enables us to see what lies at the heart of the matter and to judge what really is at stake and ought to be done. And in this respect, everyone appears wise to herself: technical matters excepted, we do not allow others to decide for us what we should believe or how we should live.

To be wise is to have a certain knack or skill, one born from experience. And so it is easy to think of it as something like riding a bicycle, which once acquired is never lost. Wisdom lingers, as Tennyson said.

But this is foolishly complacent. Wisdom is frail, and nothing shatters it more violently than the belief that it has been permanently acquired. This, more than anything else, has been the *raison d'être* of this book. We gather insights, often summed up in well-known phrases or quotations, but over time we stop thinking about them and they degenerate into empty clichés. We take them for granted, oversimplify them or miss their key point and their insight is lost, replaced by foolish misunderstandings.

To be wise is not to achieve a state of maturity from which one never regresses, but to keep one's understanding sharp by persisting in a habit of constant questioning and a refusal to take things for granted. This is not the serenity of the mythical sage but the gruelling vigilance of the mind that rejects the psychological comfort of received certainties.

Anything of value in this book will not linger of its own accord. It will endure in the minds only of those who continue to question as it has done, and better. Wisdom is not a product but a process.

Notes

1 See 'The Boundaries of Loss Aversion' by Nathan Novemsky and Daniel Kahneman, *Journal of Marketing Research*, Vol XLII (May 2005) 119–28; and 'Experimental Tests of the Endowment Effect and the Coase Theorem' by Daniel Kahneman, Jack L. Knetsch, and Richard H. Thaler, *Journal of Political Economy*, Vol. 98 (December 1990), 1325–48.

2 'Quiet! Sleeping brain at work', Robert Stickgold and Jeffrey M. Ellenborgen, *Scientific American Mind*, August/September 2008, 22–9.

3 *The Natural History*, Pliny the Elder, ed. John Bostock (www.perseus.tufts.edu).

4 'Less is more: The lure of ambiguity, or why familiarity breeds contempt', Michael I. Norton, Jeana H. Frost and Dan Ariely, *Journal of Personality and Social Psychology*, Vol. 92(1), Jan. 2007, 97–105.

5 I would have thought that this saying is much older, but the earliest attribution I could find is by *The Columbia World of Quotations* to Rose Tremain, writing in the short-lived newspaper the *Sunday Correspondent* on 24 December 1989.

6 'The neural correlates of maternal and romantic love', Andreas Bartels and Semir Zeki, *NeuroImage*, 21 (2004) 1155–66.

7 As quoted in James Boswell's *Life of Johnson* (1791).

8 *Essential Research Findings in Counselling and Psychotherapy*, Mick Cooper (London: Sage, 2008), pp. 19–20.

9 Figlio, David N., 'Names, Expectations and the Black-White Test Score Gap' (March 2005). NBER Working Paper No. W11195. Available at SSRN: http://ssrn.com/abstract=684721

Acknowledgements

Some of the chapters in this book appeared in an earlier form as part of a series called 'Wisdom's Folly', which ran in the *Guardian* from 2004 to 2005. Thanks especially to Ian Katz for incubating the concept.

Thanks as ever to the enthusiastic and supportive Granta team, especially Sara Holloway, Brigid Macleod, Christine Lo, Lindsay Paterson, Angela Rose, Pru Rowlandson and Sarah Wasley. Lizzy Kremer's guidance and judgement have been as invaluable as ever. Thanks also to Bela Cunha for her diligence and patience, and to the Faber and Faber sales team who work so hard to get my books on shelves.

Thanks most of all to Antonia, for everything.

Index

Index

Index

Index

Index

Index

Mansfield, Katherine, 152
map-reading, 182
marriage and married couples,
    19, 20, 26–7, 46, 49, 119
  haste, in, 88
  vows, 171
  women, 3
  wrong person, 9
Mars, 182
material possessions, love and,
    129–30
martyrdom, 52
Marx, Karl, 61, 65
masks, 61
matches, 7
Maugham, W. Somerset, 20, 28,
    188
McCarthy era, 99
McCartney, Paul, 129
measure of things, 139–40
medicine, 48
memorabilia, 163–4
memories, 33–4
  imperfect, 60
men and man, 31, 35
  boys' toys, 181–2
  company, and, 149–50
  deaf, 142
  drunken, 58
  manhood, 152
  manners, and, 3
  measure of things, 139–40
  meeting ladies, 3
  rapists, 101–2
  seven
    ages of, 62
    wise, 9
  travel, and, 147–8

  see also journeys
  wishes, 185–6
  women, and, 181–2
Midsummer's Night's Dream, A
    (Shakespeare), 172
Middle East, 125
Milan, 179
milk, spilt, 77–8
Mill, John Stuart, 28
Milton, John, 24
minds and brains, 31, 33, 34, 47,
    48, 87
  brain imaging, 157
  chemical imbalance in, 94
  decisions and thinking, and,
    117, 119
  dull and feeble, 91, 92, 136
  learning, and, 141, 142
  male and female brains, 182
  travel, and, 148
Minerva, 98
mines, 184
misery and misfortune *see*
    unhappiness
mistakes, 137–8, 143, 151
Mogadishu, 163
monarchies, absolute, 96
money, 37–8, 186
  lending and borrowing, 89–90
  love, and, 129–30
  see also charity; rich people
monkeys and apes, 92, 139
monks and monastic life, 45, 46,
    100
Monty Python's Life of Brian, 13
Moore, George, 147
morals, 3, 113–14, 131, 132,
    133, 139

Index